CORFE REMEMBERED

DR ANDREW NORMAN

HALSGROVE

First published in Great Britain in 2017

British Library Cataloguing-in-Publication Data
A CIP record for this title is available from the British Library

ISBN 978 0 85704 302 3

HALSGROVE
Halsgrove House,
Ryelands Industrial Estate,
Bagley Road, Wellington, Somerset TA21 9PZ
Tel: 01823 653777   Fax: 01823 216796
email: sales@halsgrove.com

Part of the Halsgrove group of companies
Information on all Halsgrove titles is available at: www.halsgrove.com

Printed and bound by Parksons Graphics, India

CONTENTS

PREFACE

Corfe Castle is one of the most popular tourist destinations in Britain. Although a ruin, the remains of its once mighty keep is visible from Poole Quay, 6 miles distant, as the crow flies. Images of it appear frequently in newspapers and magazines. On a misty day, or when it is silhouetted against the sky, there is an air of magic and mystery about it. The castle was a favourite of the infamous King John, and Lady Bankes defended it nobly for the Royalists during the English Civil War.

The village of Corfe is also of interest, with its seventeenth-century town hall – said to be the smallest in England – and which today houses a museum. There is also a model village and a railway, which offers the opportunity of a ride on a steam train. Quaint cottages and peaceful common where ponies abide, are also an attraction. Famous visitors include John Wesley, Thomas Hardy, and Kaiser Wilhelm II.

Not so long ago, this was a world of horse and plough; performing bear; scissor and knife grinder, and muffin man.

*Some modern-day Cavaliers
parading at Corfe.*

ACKNOWLEDGEMENTS

My sincere thanks to all the wonderful people of Corfe Castle and elsewhere who have made this book possible.

Liz Agnew; Jennifer S. Barnard; Nigel W. E. Baynes; Leslie Everett Baynes; Barbara Cannings; Stephen Dru Drury; Jim Fooks; Louise Haywood; Reverend Ian Jackson; Barry King; Joyce Meates; Ed Paris; Bob Pugh; Jessica Sutcliffe; Cindy Ramm; Bob and Liz Richards; Trish and Alan Sherwood; Mary Wills.

And I am deeply grateful to my beloved wife Rachel for all her help and encouragement.

ABOUT THE AUTHOR

Andrew Norman was born in Newbury, Berkshire, UK in 1943. Having been educated at Thornhill High School, Gwelo, Southern Rhodesia (now Zimbabwe), Midsomer Norton Grammar School, and St Edmund Hall, Oxford, he qualified in medicine at the Radcliffe Infirmary. He has two children Bridget and Thomas, by his first wife.

From 1972-83, Andrew worked as a general practitioner in Poole, Dorset, before a spinal injury cut short his medical career. He is now an established writer whose published works include biographies of Charles Darwin, Winston Churchill, Thomas Hardy, T.E. Lawrence, Adolf Hitler, Agatha Christie, Enid Blyton, Beatrix Potter, Sir Arthur Conan Doyle, and Robert Mugabe. Andrew married his second wife Rachel, in 2005.

BY THE SAME AUTHOR

By Swords Divided: Corfe Castle in the Civil War. Halsgrove, 2003.
Dunshay: Reflections on a Dorset Manor House. Halsgrove, 2004.
Sir Francis Drake: Behind the Pirate's Mask. Halsgrove, 2004.
Thomas Hardy: Christmas Carollings. Halsgrove, 2005.
Enid Blyton and her Enchantment with Dorset. Halsgrove, 2005.
Agatha Christie: The Finished Portrait. Tempus, 2007.
Tyneham: A Tribute. Halsgrove, 2007.
Mugabe: Teacher, Revolutionary, Tyrant. The History Press, 2008.
T. E. Lawrence: The Enigma Explained. The History Press, 2008.
The Story of George Loveless and the Tolpuddle Martyrs. Halsgrove, 2008.
Father of the Blind: A Portrait of Sir Arthur Pearson. The History Press, 2009.
Agatha Christie: The Finished Portrait. Tempus, 2006.
Agatha Christie: The Pitkin Guide. Pitkin Publishing, 2009.
Jane Austen: An Unrequited Love. The History Press, 2009.
Arthur Conan Doyle: The Man behind Sherlock Holmes. The History Press, 2009.
HMS Hood: Pride of the Royal Navy. The History Press, 2009.
Purbeck Personalities. Halsgrove, 2009.
Bournemouth's Founders and Famous Visitors. The History Press, 2010.
Jane Austen: An Unrequited Love. The History Press, 2009.
Thomas Hardy: Behind the Mask. The History Press, 2011.
Hitler: Dictator or Puppet. Pen & Sword Books, 2011.
A Brummie Boy goes to War. Halsgrove, 2011.
Winston Churchill: Portrait of an Unquiet Mind. Pen & Sword Books, 2012.
Charles Darwin: Destroyer of Myths. Pen & Sword Books, 2013.
Beatrix Potter: Her Inner World. Pen & Sword Books, 2013.
T.E. Lawrence: Tormented Hero. Fonthill, 2014.
Agatha Christie: The Disappearing Novelist. Fonthill, 2014.
Lawrence of Arabia's Clouds Hill. Halsgrove, 2014.
Kindly Light: The Story of Blind Veterans UK. Fonthill, 2015.
Jane Austen: Love is Like a Rose. Fonthill, 2015.
Thomas Hardy at Max Gate: The Latter Years. Halsgrove, 2016.

Author's website www.andrew-norman.com

One
THE ENVIRONS OF CORFE

The name 'Corfe' derives from the Old English word 'Ceorfan', meaning 'to cut'. This reflects the fact that Corfe is situated in a cutting, or gap, in the line of the Purbeck hills. The promontory on which the castle stands is a natural one, with the Corfe River (or River Wicken) running around its north, west, and south side, and the Byle Brook around its east side. In this narrative, Corfe refers to the village and Corfe Castle, to the castle. Although Corfe was traditionally referred to as a town, today it is usually referred to as a village.

Evidence of prehistoric life abounds in Purbeck. During the Late Triassic (227-205 mya – million years ago), the Jurassic (205-144 mya) and the Cretaceous (144-65 mya) eras, dinosaurs roamed the Earth. And one of the joys of living in South Dorsetshire's so-called 'Jurassic Coast', is that their fossilized remains are frequently being discovered.

In 1933 local archaeologist J. B. Calkin recorded the discovery of 14 footprints of the dinosaur *Iguanodon*, at Suttle's Quarry, Herston, near Swanage. When palaeontologists from the British Museum visited the site, more footprints, believed to be those of a *Megalosaurus*, were discovered.[1] Part of this 'dinosaur trackway' is currently on display in London, at the Natural History Museum's 'Wildlife Garden'.

In 1981, D. W. Selby of Townsend, Swanage, discovered in his garden, numerous footprints of 3-toed dinosaurs, believed to have been made by a *Megalosaurus* and an *Iguanodon*.

In 1997 on a plateau of Purbeck limestone covering an area of approximately 1 acre, numerous dinosaur footprints were found at Keates' quarry, Worth Matravers. The prints were made by a *Sauropod*, weighing in at 10 tons or more!

At the, so-called, 'Fossil Forest' at Lulworth are to be found the fossilized remains of cycads – giant ferns – dating from about 140 mya. They were therefore contemporary with the dinosaurs. Fossilized remains of crocodiles, turtles, lizards, and pterosaurs – winged reptiles – have also been discovered.

Fossilized ammonites, up to 3 feet in diameter, are the remains of ammonoids – extinct molluscs of the Jurassic and Cretaceous eras. They are so plentiful in Purbeck that people build them into the walls of their houses as decorative features.

The following artifacts, found in Purbeck, date from the times indicated.

Flints used by Cro-Magnons (the first early modern humans, who first arrived in Britain about 42,000 years ago) were used as arrowheads to sharpen wooden tools, or to cut up meat. Subsequently, from about 23,000 years ago, man virtually disappeared from the British landscape, when, with the Last Glacial Period (or 'Ice Age'), ice covered northern and central England, Scotland, Ireland, and most of Wales. Around 14,000 BCE (before the Common Era), rising sea levels caused by the melting of the ice led to Ireland being separated from Great Britain. In about 14,700 BCE, man returned to Britain. In about 5600 BCE, continuing rise in sea level led Great Britain to become separated from mainland Europe.

The early farmers of the Stone Age (or Neolithic period, which in Northern Europe dates from circa 4000 BCE to 2500 BCE – 2000 BCE) slashed and burned the forests, to create the fields for grazing and growing crops. This was the fate of Corfe Common. However, this land soon became unproductive and reverted to heathland.

Artifacts dating from this period have been found on the Purbeck Hills. For example, an axe was discovered on Ballard Down, and a single long barrow (ancient burial mound), aligned from east to west in the customary way, is to be found on what later became known as Nine Barrow Down.

The stone circle at Rempstone was probably erected by the 'Beaker Folk' of the Bronze Age (circa 2500 BCE to circa 800 BCE), who arrived in Britain circa 1800 BCE. They were so called because they produced distinctive pottery beakers, shaped like inverted bells. They also built a number of round barrows on Nine Barrow Down, in which their hierarchy were buried; lying on their sides in a crouched position, with crockery for use in the afterlife.

Immigrant Celts (pre-Roman inhabitants of much of Europe and Asia Minor, speaking the Celtic language) arrived in about 1000 BCE from across the Channel, bringing with them bronze tools and weapons. In about 450 BCE more Celts arrived: this time with superior tools and weapons made of iron. The Celts built hill forts: the most notable in Dorsetshire being Maiden Castle near Dorchester, which became the capital of the Celtic Durotriges tribe. When the Romans conquered Britain in 43 CE (Common Era), however, they defeated the Durotriges and captured Maiden Castle.[2]

In 1975, Tony Brown of Corfe encountered some molehills in a field belonging to Bucknowle Farm, situated half a mile to the south-west of the village, in which fragments of Roman pottery were embedded. The site was duly excavated. It revealed the presence of an Iron Age (circa 800 BCE to 100 CE) farm, together with a substantial Roman villa complex built around a central courtyard, and a farm dating from the first century. From the late fourth century, these buildings fell into disrepair. A decorated length of bone, possibly the handle of a knife and dating from the middle Iron Age (500-300 BCE), was discovered on the site. A number of Iron Age brooches were also found.

Prior to the Roman conquest, Dorsetshire was occupied by the Durotriges, a tribe which farmed, built hill forts, manufactured its own pottery, and buried its dead in the traditional crouched position, together with crockery presumably for use in the afterlife. In a grave at Bucknowle was discovered a female skeleton in just such a position (together with six Durotrigian pottery vessels). For some unknown reason, her lower jaw was missing. Among the 200, or so, coins found at Bucknowle was a silver Durotrigian 'stater', dating from between 60 BCE and 20 CE.

As for the succeeding Romans, they engaged in fulling (cleansing wool), tanning leather, and fashioning Kimmeridge shale into rings, bracelets, armlets, bowls and furniture for distribution throughout Britain.

On a Roman rubbish dump at Bucknowle, the following artifacts were discovered: a broken glass jug, which was probably imported by the Romans from the Rhineland in the second century; two fine, glossy, reddish-brown Samian pottery jars with incised, rather than moulded decoration – Samian ware being extensively used in Roman Britain; a female face cast in bronze, and intended to be hung on a wall or door, which may represent a goddess, either Roman or local; a bronze brooch, dating from the second century and decorated with orange, red, green, and blue enamel; Roman coins in silver and bronze; a small, gold, Gallo–Belgic 'quarter-stater' dating from about 70 BCE.

One of the main rooms at Bucknowle Roman Villa included a hypocaust, a form of underfloor central heating whereby hot air from a furnace is drawn under the flagstones of the floor, which are supported at intervals by blocks of chalk. The Roman bath suite situated at the east end of the villa, comprised a hot room, cold room, and cold bath 'with a mysterious, deep, paved room to the west of the hot room'.[3] The 'Drying Room', which was presumably where corn and other foodstuffs were dried, prior to being stored, also included a hypocaust system.

Two

NOTABLE EVENTS WHICH OCCURRED AT CORFE DURING THE REIGNS OF VARIOUS MONARCHS

Corfe Castle was of strategic importance to the monarchs of England from at least as early as the ninth century, until the seventeenth century. Over this period, its defences were strengthened, so as to make it virtually impregnable, as will now be seen.

Alfred (King of Wessex, Ruled 871-899)
Said George Bankes (1787-1856), descendant of Sir John Bankes of Kingston Lacy

> *There is reason for concluding that a castle existed at Corfe in the reign of King Alfred. A presumption to this effect arises from the undoubted fact that he was founder of the Abbey of Shaftesbury, with which religious endowment this castle was constantly connected in the periods of our early history. Ethelgiva, daughter of King Alfred, was the first Abbess of Shaftesbury, and to her and her successors, high rights and privileges were granted connected with Corfe Castle and the surrounding domain.*
>
> *Alfred had a little leisure for the enjoyments of a palace. This structure, which afterwards became so large as to vie with the noblest royal habitations in the kingdom, consisted in his time, probably, of only a single strong tower on the summit of the hill, constituting one of the defences of Wareham [often described as 'The Gateway to Purbeck'], which in Saxon times was a very principal town and port, against the depredations of the Danish and other pagan nations.[1]*

Bankes describes how, in 875, Alfred made an agreement with the Danes that they be assigned 'a large portion of the northern provinces of the kingdom', and having done so, 'flattered himself with the enjoyment of some repose'. However, Alfred's repose was not to last, for in the spring of that year

> *Halfden, a Danish general, with a very considerable force took by surprise Wareham Castle, then the strongest place in all Wessex.[2]*

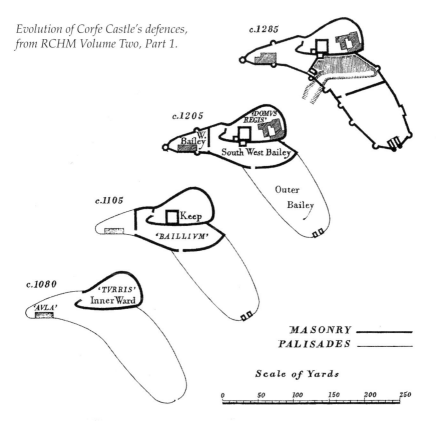

Evolution of Corfe Castle's defences, from RCHM Volume Two, Part 1.

Having remonstrated with the Danes to no effect, Alfred raised an army

> *with which he engaged the enemy seven times in one campaign. Fortune was not equally favourable to him in all these engagements, but the king succeeded in rendering their residence at Wareham so little commodious to them, that in the year 877 the army of pagans quitted Wareham, partly on horseback and partly by water.*[3]

A fortress was now constructed at Corfe

> *to effect a security against their return at some future time. Whatever may have been the size or construction of this castle in the days of King Alfred, it was greatly extended and embellished in the century next following, under the direction of the magnificent King Edgar. This splendid monarch procured from Italy workmen to instruct and aid the native artisans.*[4]

11

Corfe, plan. Photo: Lillian Ladle and Keith Jarvis

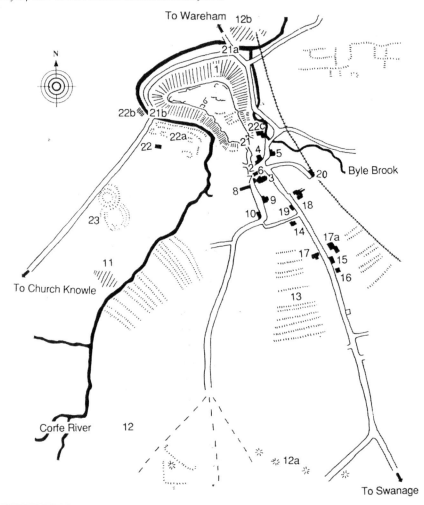

1. The Castle	12. Corfe Common	19. The Old Forge
2. Market Square	12a. Barrow on Corfe Common	20. Railway Station
3. St Edward's Church	12b. Norden Iron Age Site	21. Castle Bridge
4. Greyhound Hotel	13. The Hawes	21a. St Edward's Bridge
5. Uvedale House	14. Congregational Church	21b. Corfe River Bridge
6. Town House	15. Almshouse	22. The Vineyard
7. Town Hall	16. Castle Inn	22a. Remains of Medieval Fishponds
8. Fox Inn	17. Old National School	22b. Site of West Mill
9. Post Office	(now British Legion)	22c. Boar Mill
10. The Old Bakery	17a. Corfe Castle First School	23. The Rings
11. Bucknowle Roman Villa	18. Mortons House	

Edgar (King of England 959-975)
Edgar died in 975, having bequeathed Corfe Castle to his (second) wife Elfrida, as a 'dowry mansion'. (Dowry – a widow's life interest in her husband's estate.[5]) This was to have fatal consequences for King Edward, his successor and son by his first wife Ethelfleda.[6]

William I (1066-1087)
Corfe Castle's keep, at this time, was probably made of timber. The perimeter boundaries of the castle were similar to that which exists today. However, in William's time, only the inner bailey (or 'ward' i.e compartment surrounded by a wall), containing keep and royal apartments – 'Domus Regis' – was enclosed by a 'curtain [fortified stone] wall', the remainder being enclosed by a wooden palisade.[7] William I was succeeded by William II (1087-1100)

Henry I (1100-1135)
It is generally accepted that it was Henry who ordered the building of the castle's first stone keep in circa 1105, during the early years of his reign.[8]

> *It was constructed from Purbeck, broken shell limestone, hauled across Corfe Common from open-cast quarries 2 or 3 miles away to the south, using horses and carts or sledges.[9]*

Beneath the basement of the keep lay the dungeons. In Henry's reign, the south-west bailey's surrounding wooden palisade was replaced by a curtain wall, 10 to 12 feet thick.[10]

In 1106, Henry fought in France in the Battle of Tinchebrai, against his eldest brother Robert, Duke of Normandy. Robert was captured and imprisoned at Corfe, prior to being sent to Cardiff Castle, where he died in 1134.

Stephen (1135-1154)
Situated 300 yards, or so, to the west of the castle is a ring-and-bailey castle, known as 'The Rings'. This was a fortification with a keep and bailey standing atop a raised earthwork, surrounded by a protective palisade and ditch, the remains of which can be seen today. It is believed to have been built by King Stephen in 1139 at a time of rebellion, followed by civil war, when Corfe Castle was seized by the powerful baron, Baldwin de Redvers. Operating from The Rings, Stephen besieged the castle, but was unsuccessful.

During the reigns of Stephen's successors – Henry II (1154-1189) and Richard I (1189-1199) – no material additions to the castle were made.

John (1199-1216)

Corfe Castle was a favourite of King John, who lavished considerable sums of money on it. The *Gloriette* was built – 'a luxurious palace with a highly-decorated great chamber, bedrooms, and other state rooms, above a vaulted undercroft'.[11]

The King sent 15 of his own miners and stonemasons to remove the curtain wall between the south-west bailey and the outer bailey, and resite it on the south side of a great ditch, which they now proceeded to create.[12]

Repairs were made to 'the houses of the castle' i.e. 'to the several buildings within the fortifications, exclusive of the keep and the 'other towers which have specific names'.[13] The timber palisade surrounding the west bailey was replaced by a curtain wall,[14] which linked round towers complete with arrow slits from which archers could fire down on any would-be intruder who attempted to climb the steep banks below. Along the top of the walls ran fortified walkways.

John made frequent visits to Corfe Castle. Here, he kept his treasure, the coronation crown, and much of the precious jewellery that he was so fond of collecting. He also hunted in the royal warren.

In 1202, John took an army to France and besieged the Castle of Mirambeau near Bordeaux: capturing Arthur, Duke of Brittany, claimant to the English throne; his sister Eleanor; and numerous French knights. Arthur and Eleanor were the offspring of John's brother, the late Geoffrey, Duke of Brittany. Arthur disappeared, presumably having been murdered, and Eleanor was imprisoned at Corfe, as were 24 of the knights, 22 of whom were starved to death[15] – probably in an *oubliette* – a windowless dungeon into which prisoners could be thrown and forgotten about. (From the Middle French, 'oublier' – 'to forget'.)

When King William of Scotland's daughter became engaged to the Earl of Boulogne, without King John's approval, the latter 'summoned the King of Scots to answer for his presumption', and in 1209 'marched a powerful army into Scotland to enforce the demand'. The outcome was that William

> *in order to appease a powerful neighbour, delivered his daughters into the hands of the King of England, at whose pleasure they were to be disposed of in marriage.[16]*

The daughters were Marjery and Isabel: they were imprisoned at Corfe until John's successor Henry III, came to the throne, when they were released and married-off to English noblemen.

During their confinement, the two Scottish princesses, together with King John's niece Eleanor (who persisted with her claim to the English throne), were treated well; dined on the King's venison, and were supplied with clothing of the highest quality, including tunic, super tunics, capes of cambric, furs of minerver, robes, caps, and pairs of boots. Eleanor 'was provided with a beautiful saddle with scarlet ornaments and gilded reins', which implies that she was allowed to go riding.[17]

In 1213 the hermit Peter de Pomfret, was

> *by the King's command, dragged by horses about the town of Corfe, together with his sons, and then hanged.*[18]

De Pomfret's 'crime' had been to predict that King John would not reign for more than fourteen years. In fact, John reigned for seventeen years. Others to be imprisoned by King John at Corfe were his second wife Queen Isabella, various hostages sent by the King of Scotland, and some rebellious barons.

On a happier note, in 1215 permission was given by King John for a regular market to be held at Corfe – hence, the name, 'Market Place' (now known as 'The Square').

In 1216, William Longspée, Earl of Salisbury and half-brother of King John, who had been captured two years earlier by King Philip II of France at the Battle of Bouvines, was exchanged for Robert, Count de Dreaux, who was John's prisoner at Corfe.[19]

During the last twelve years of his life, prior to his death in 1216, John

> *frequently visited Corfe Castle, but his stay was often limited to a single day, and seldom extended beyond four or five, excepting in the last year, when he remained here from the 23 June to the 17 July. His last visit was on the 25 August, and was limited to that and the following day.*[20]

In about 1222, Eleanor was transferred to other prisons – Gloucester, Malborough, and finally Bristol – 'where she is said to have passed the rest of her wearisome existence'.[21]

Henry III (1216-1272)
Henry was staying at Corfe Castle with his mother Isabella of Angoulême, when his father King John, died. During his 'minority' (1216-1226, before he was deemed old enough to rule)

> *many of the great barons usurped the king's castles and other possessions of the crown, which they refused to surrender to legitimate authority.*

One such 'refractory noble' was Peter de Mauley, who, in 1221 was taken prisoner and only freed when he surrendered Corfe Castle to the King, complete with its prisoners, and 'all the jewels, military engines, and ammunition therein.'[22]

When the rebellious Simon de Montfort, Earl of Leicester, was killed at the battle of Evesham in 1265, his son Almeric, was subsequently imprisoned at Corfe.

As for the fabric of the castle itself, Henry lavished care and money on it; just as his father King John had done before him. The houses of the castle; its turrets, drawbridge, and well, were repaired, and wooden palisades replaced with stone walls. To this end timber was brought, by sea, from Southampton to the nearest port (which was Ower on the southern shore of Poole Harbour). For his work, Gerard the carpenter was paid 7¼d (pence) per day.

In 1246, the tower (presumably the interior) was plastered with mortar and whitewashed.[23] In 1250, the south-west gatehouse was built.[24] In 1261, the Sheriff of Dorset and Somerset was

commanded to make a stable in a convenient place within the castle of Corfe, large enough for 20 horses, and to repair the gates and bridges of the castle without delay.[25]

The semi-circular tower on the eastern side of the outer bailey bears a coat-of-arms which is believed to be that of the Plukenet family. As Alan de Plukenet was constable of the castle from 1270 to 1272, the tower presumably dates from this period.

In 1277, stone was mined from a quarry at Holme near Wareham. This was dark, red sandstone, similar to that of which the so-called 'Butavant Tower' is composed. This tower, therefore, probably dates from this period.

In 1281, Adam Bureis was paid 5s. (shillings) 'for making two great hinges and hooks for the outer gate, and nails for the same; and master Ralph de Totewys was paid 2s. for preparing the places where the hinges should be put, and for cutting the stone'. A tiler was employed to maintain the roofs of the King and Queen's chambers, the chapel, the *gloriette*

and over the gate before the great tower, and over the other houses, when necessary. Three men and four women received 12d. for cleaning out the prison, called the 'Swalwe', and at the same time 5¼d. was paid for cleaning out the prison called 'Malemit'. A woman who brought 'mosse' to put under the lead received 4d. [The 'mosse' referred to was presumably moss, for lining the roofs and providing insulation.] Master William the plumber, was paid 20s. for leading two towers.

In 1282 'a boy was paid 1¼d. for going to Cerne, Godmanston and

Dorchester, in quest of carpenters'. 3d. was paid 'for a cord made at Stodland [Studland] for dragging timber. '21d. was paid 'for three-quarters of lime [a constituent of lime mortar] bought at Bindon'.

For four cords made of hemp bought for raising the bridges of the castle, 7s.6d. For five locks bought for the four gates of the castle, and for the wine cellar, 2s.7d. For stone bought of Thomas Cusyn for the towers, which are called Butavant, Cokayngue [Cockayne], and Plente, ixs [9 shillings].

The cost of roofing these three towers with lead was a colossal 18l. (pounds) 3s.8d. A painter was paid 6s.8d. 'for whitening, &c the chamber of the King and Queen'.[26]

Edward I (1272-1307)
In 1280, the outer gatehouse was constructed, in stone,[27] In order to gain entrance through the outer gatehouse, it would have been necessary firstly, to evade the archers as they fired through the arrow slits of the twin towers, or down from the ramparts. The next obstacle was the 'murder hole' – through which the defenders dropped boulders, hot coals, excrement, etc., down from above. Next, there was the portcullis, and beyond it the great door, bolted and secured by a sturdy drawbar. Finally, there were the guards from the guardrooms on either side to contend with. A similar daunting task would confront those who attacked the south-west gatehouse.[28]

In King Edward's reign the outer bailey was enclosed by a curtain wall of stone,[29] linking six integral towers. The towers on the east side of the outer bailey were named 'Plukenet' and 'Horseshoe'. The names of three of the four towers on the west side were 'Cockayne', 'Plente', and 'Sauvery' (The name of the fourth tower is not known).[30]

In 1306, Walter de Morreve, a follower of Robert the Bruce, King of Scotland, was detained at Corfe Castle.

Edward II (1307-1327)
In 1322, Sir John de Latimer, Constable of Corfe Castle, recorded daily payments as follows, to the following

Sixteen balistarii or crossbow men, had 4d; ten bowmen, 2d. four men-at-arms 12d. per diem [day] each. Besides these, every tything [portion of land on which a tithe was payable] of Purbeck being bound to furnish one efficient man at the king's cost, for ten days, in time of disturbance, for defence of the castle; thirty-four such men, of whom six were balistarii and eight foot lancers, received pay at the same rate as the above. Twelve men of the town of Corfe had ½d. a night for keeping watch and ward [guardianship] for forty nights, according to ancient custom.[31]

In 1325, Sir Robert de Walkefare, 'a man of crafty and turbulent disposition', was imprisoned at Corfe. However, he murdered the keeper – prison governor – and escaped to the Continent'.[32]

Edward's survey of the castle, conducted in 1326, revealed widespread damage and decay. For example: to the King's Hall, the Cockayne Tower, the Chapel of St Mary, the Long Hall, 'a certain chamber called Le Parlour', the keep, 'with the chambers and gard[e]robes [toilets and wardrobes] of the same, and the great gateways'. Also, 'the lead in divers places of the castle were carried away [i.e. missing] to the damage of 20l. [pounds]'.

Edward's rule was plagued with rebellions. Finally, on 14 November 1326 he himself was captured in Wales by rebellious barons, and imprisoned in Corfe Castle in the charge of Sir John Matravers. Edward was subsequently murdered at Berkeley Castle, Gloucestershire, on 21 September 1327.

Edward III (1327-1377)
Edward paid occasional visits to the castle.[33] In 1341 the walls of the castle were said to be 'ruinous and required extensive repairs'.

In the 1360s, a prison called 'Botevant' is mentioned, which presumably refers to the Butavant Tower. In 1368, the roof of the keep was renewed with timber and lead, and the Cockayne and Plente Towers were repaired, and their roofs re-leaded.

Richard II (1377-1399)
The *Le Gloriette* tower was built (inner bailey). At about this time, glazing was installed in the castle.

In 1381, at the request of King Richard, a jury was summoned

> *to inquire what possessions, rents, rights, customs, and liberties from ancient times belonged and then still belonged to the castle and lordship of Corfe.*

From the determinations of the jury it is clear that the reigning monarch, and the current constable of the castle, were the principal beneficiaries of the privileges referred to above. It was stated

> *That the whole Isle of Purbeck is a warren [enclosed piece of land set aside for breeding game*[34]*] of our lord the King, and pertains to his said castle.*
> *That the whole town of Corfe belongs to the said castle, and the tenants of the same town are called 'barons' [persons who held lands or property*

from the sovereign or a powerful overlord[35]], and ought to choose amongst themselves a mayor, coroner, and bailiffs, for whom they are willing to answer, and they are as free as the barons of the Cinque Ports [confederation of five coastal towns in Kent and Sussex, created for military and trading purposes].

That all pleas [trials, for offences of stealing] of vert [green forest vegetation] and venison, and also of wreck of sea, belong to the said castle.

That the tenants of the town of Corfe ought to find a cart every Saturday to carry bread and beer from Wareham to Corfe for the use of the constable.

That the constable in the King's right, in respect of the said castle, has taken, time out of mind [time immemorial], prisage [the right of the King to take a proportion of every cargo] of wine of every ship coming to the sea coast of Purbeck, if it shall remain there, and shall have been moored there with cables and anchors, and if it shall have a freight or cargo of wine.

That our lord the King has taken, time out of mind, all royal fish, viz. grampuses, porpoises, and sturgeons, caught upon the coast. That our lord the King also takes all falcons building and nesting within the said bailiwick [area of jurisdiction], but the constable is accustomed to reward the captors of such fish and falcons.

Falcons were highly prized, falconry being the skill of keeping birds of prey and training them to hunt.[36]

That common pastures everywhere within the liberty [or 'hundred' – subdivision of a county or shire having its own court] of Corfe, together with vacant lands, belong to the tenants of the said town for their common use, and also the tenants shall have of the constable every night four lagens ['lagan' – unit of measure for liquids] of beer whilst they shall keep watch within the castle in time of war.

The maior [mayor] of Corffe hath used to hunt by custome the deare [deer] or any other game yearlye upon Maye [May] daye, accompayned with his brethern [brethren] the maisters [masters] of the towne, inheretours [inheritors – possessors as of right] of the island [of Purbeck] and other gent. [gentlemen] of the countrey w^ch [which] shall happen to come, in all places of the south syde [side] of the castle and great downe [down].

Under the heading of 'Certaine Customes and Orders belonging to the Castle to be approved by the Court Rolles [Rolls – record kept by a manorial court of rent paid and property held by tenants] and com'on [common] use', it is stated that

The constable, officer, and steward may keepe every iiij^th [fourth] weekes a

courte called hundred courte, wherein are tryed [tried] wrytts [writs] of right, pleas of trespass and debt, and all other common pleas.

And under the heading, 'Other Customes and Orders approved by the Courts Rolles' it is stated that

No ilander [islander] ought to marye [marry off] his daughter oute of [outside of] the island without license of the lord constable or other officer.

That no inhabitant of the ilande shall make any stone wall, hedge, or dyche [ditch] above the assysse [above the height allowed by court regulations], that is no higher than that a hinde with her calf may easely leape over at all places.

That no man ought to take or hunt any coneys, hare, ffox [fox], or ffeasaunt [pheasant] with dogges [dogs], nettes, of ferryatts [ferrets] within the warren, without license or vewe [presumably personal knowledge] of the warrener [gamekeeper].

That no inheritor of the ilande may keepe, carry, or lead lose [set loose] any dogges [dogs] or curres [curs] in the heath or elsewhere, to the disturbaunce of the game, or to drive them out of their pastures.

That no man ought to take any ffishe [fish] on the Saboth [Sabbath] Daye.

That all ilanders ought sufficiently to fence their woods; and that they ought to keepe out their cattayle [cattle] out of their woods.[37]

From the above it is clear a), that the powers-that-be attached great importance to the preservation of Purbeck as a royal hunting warren, and that b), the constable of the castle had virtually complete jurisdiction over its inhabitants.

Finally, the late fourteenth century was a period when the more important castles were first being supplied with artillery.[38]

Richard II was succeeded by Henry IV, V, and VI, Edward IV and V, Richard III, and Henry VII.

Henry VII (1485-1509)

The King was granted £2000 by Parliament for repairs to the castle, in order that it should serve as a home for his mother Margaret, Countess of Richmond.

The manor and castle, which always went together, were often granted to princes of the blood [i.e. those who were legitimately descended in dynastic line from a former monarch of the realm] and the favourites of our kings.[39]

Henry VII was succeeded by Henry VIII, Edward VI, Mary I, and Elizabeth I.

Elizabeth I (1558-1603)

In 1572, the Queen sold Corfe Castle and its estate to Christopher Hatton, Esquire, 'then one of her gentleman pensioners', for the price of £4761 18s 7½d. Hatton 'afterwards became conspicuous as Sir Christopher Hatton, the Lord Chancellor'.[40]

In that same year of 1572, Hatton obtained from the Queen a charter, which conferred upon

> *the inhabitants of the Castle and borough… all the same rights and privileges as those enjoyed by the inhabitants and barons of the Cinque Ports, including the right of returning two members to Parliament.*[41]

The first two members of Parliament (MPs) for Corfe Castle, who were returned in that year of 1572, were Sir Edmund Uvedale, Esquire, of Gussage All Saints and Holt Park, Dorsetshire; and Charles Matthews, Esquire.[42]

In the 1580s, when England was threatened by war with Spain, the defences of Corfe Castle were strengthened.

> *Near the King's Tower, was a semicircular platform, over which, in 1586, were five pieces of cannon mounted.*[43]

The Spanish Armada duly sailed up the English Channel in 1588, but was defeated.

Elizabeth I was succeeded by James I, Charles I, Charles II, James II, William of Orange, William III, Anne, George I, George II.

George III (1760-1801)

Historically, West Street was Corfe's main thoroughfare, leading northwards to Wareham and southwards across Corfe Common to Lynch, Kingston, Langton Matravers, and Swanage. As for East Street, this terminated at its southern end in the hamlet of Town's End, beyond which was a bog.

In 1765 the road from Wareham to Swanage, via Corfe and Kingston, became a turnpike (road on which a toll was collected), and here and there at the roadside, a milestone dating from those times can still be seen. The bog was drained, and a new road created between East Street and Kingston, via Lynch. And it was probably at about this time that the route of East Street was changed so that it now ran along the east side of Boar Mill and the Byle

Brook, and not the west. East Street now became Corfe's main thoroughfare. In the 1840s, the turnpike system came to an end.

George III was succeeded by George IV and William IV.

William IV (1830-1837)
In 1832, the right of Corfe to return two MPs was revoked by the Reform Bill: this being deemed a 'rotten borough' (one with was able to elect an MP, despite having very few voters). In 1833 the posts of mayor and corporation were abolished.

William IV was succeeded by Queen Victoria, Edward VII, and George V.

George V (1910-1936)
In the late 1920s the Valley Road was built, linking Corfe to Swanage via Harman's Cross. This was a more direct route than via Kingston.

Three
THE PURBECK MARBLE INDUSTRY

Purbeck marble is so called because it is only to be found within Dorset-shire's Isle of Purbeck. As for the marble industry, which flourished in Corfe in former times, it now exists only in the hearts, minds, and workshops of a handful of local potters.

Purbeck marble is a sedimentary, fossiliferous limestone (unlike true marble which is metamorphic), created during the late Jurassic/early Cretaceous period of history, i.e. about 145 million years ago, when dinosaurs abounded and birds were beginning to evolve. The sedimentation occurred in a huge, freshwater lake, which is believed to have occupied an area between the present day Isle of Wight and Dorchester, Dorsetshire's county town.

Purbeck marble is composed of ooliths – spherical particles consisting of shell fragments – which gathered concentric layers of calcium carbonate around themselves as they rolled around on the bed of the lake. The shells are those of the tiny, freshwater snail, *Viviparus*. Over the ages, this agglomeration was geomorphically changed, by the action of heat and pressure, into a crystalline substance – Purbeck marble. When polished, the marble attains a glorious and lustrous sheen; the fossilized shells on its shiny surface being clearly visible to the naked eye. The colour of the ooliths varies from pale cream or buff, pink, and blue-grey; hence the observed variation in the colour of the marble.

The seam of Purbeck marble runs in a gentle arc between Peveril Point (a rocky outcrop on the south side of Swanage Bay), westwards to Worbarrow Tout on the east side of Worbarrow Bay – a distance of about 10 miles. The nearest point to Corfe Castle at which the seam has been mined is Blashen-well, 1½ miles distant.

The lateral width of the outcrop is influenced by 'secondary folding' i.e. distortion of the Earth's crust, causing dipping down, rising up, and dipping down again. However, evidence from medieval mine working reveals that the outcrop can extend to 80 yards, or so, in width.

As regards the depth of the seam, along the central part of the outcrop there are three layers. They are, in descending order: blue, green, and grey; each one roughly 2-feet thick and separated by layers of softer marine clays and mudstone. Objects made of Purbeck marble are therefore limited in size to not more than this thickness.

It is likely that many, if not most, of the small settlements which are located along the length of the Purbeck marble seam, originated as mining communities. They are, travelling from east to west from Pevcril Point: Swanage, Herston, Wilkswood, Quarr, Haycrafts, Dunshay, Afflington, Scoles, Lynch, Lynch West and Blashenwell. At all these locations the marble seam lies near to the surface, thus enabling open-cast mining to take place.

The Romans were aware of the existence of Purbeck marble, and they made good use of it. For example, for (inscribed) memorial tablets, examples of which have been found in France as well as in England; for architectural and decorative veneers; also, because of its hardness and durability, for pestles and mortars, and for grindstones.[1] It was also used in the Roman 'fashion industry' in the manufacture of 'amulets' – ornamental objects to protect against evil, danger, or disease.[2] However, it was not until the coming of the Normans in the eleventh century that the marble was extensively exploited.

Following the Norman conquest of 1066, Purbeck marble was hauled from the quarries overland on wooden sledges drawn by oxen to Corfe, where it was 'dressed' (fashioned). The ancient trackways, which thus became etched into the landscape, can be seen to this very day. Such was the scale of the industry that according to local historian, antiquarian, and author of *The History and Antiquities of the County of Dorset* (1861-1873), the Reverend John Hutchins, the marble chippings which piled up in Corfe's West Street – in those days the village's main thoroughfare – grew to a depth of 10 feet! Corfe soon became the centre of the marble industry, and marblers migrated here from London: amongst them Edmund Corfe, Peter Corfe, Hugo de Corfe and John de Corfe. (the appellation 'Corfe', or 'de Corfe', was presumably a reflection of the fact that this is where these skilled artisans now lived.)

From Corfe, the Purbeck marble was taken on in similar fashion to Ower Quay on the southern shores of Poole Harbour, where it was loaded onto flat-bottomed barges – 'lighters' – which conveyed it to cargo ships waiting in the South Deep Channel. These, in turn, transported it to various locations around the coast.

As Hutchins stated, Purbeck marble was used extensively in ecclesiastical buildings, particularly in southern England, for columns and monumental slabs. However, because the seam of marble is fragmented, the length of the columns produced was restricted, in general, to between 7 feet and 10 feet.[3]

Purbeck marble from the quarries at Dunshay, for example, was shipped from Poole Harbour, 12 miles eastwards to Christchurch Harbour in Hampshire, and thence up the River Avon to Harnham Quay, from where it was taken overland the further mile, or so, to the construction site at Salisbury, where a magnificent new cathedral was being built.

Was all Purbeck marble fashioned at Corfe? Evidently not. The late Mary Spencer Watson of Dunshay Manor, for example, possessed a collection of fragments, which she had found locally. This included columns of Purbeck marble, which had been accidentally fractured in the manufacturing process, and a column plinth.

Mary Spencer Watson also discovered at Dunshay Manor, some dark, rounded, pebble-like stones, each of which was of a size that would fit comfortably into the palm of an adult's hand. Made of iron gritstone, they were formerly used with sand and water to polish the marble.[4] Some, at least, of the work of polishing the Purbeck marble was therefore performed 'on-site' at Dunshay, probably under the supervision of expert stonemasons, who would have travelled up the valley from Corfe: the castle being clearly visible from the rear of Dunshay Manor.

What is not properly understood, even to this day, is how the Purbeck marble was cut longitudinally and shaped into perfectly straight columns, given the fact that this is an extremely hard substance to work. It is, therefore, difficult to imagine a tool of sufficient sharpness and durability by means of which such a task could have been accomplished.

Purbeck marble was employed in the 234-foot long nave of Salisbury's cathedral, as exterior decoration for its supporting columns. Slimmer columns still, either in clusters or singly, are to be found above, in the piers of the arcades of the triforium, and higher still in the clerestory. Marble columns, plinths and capitals also adorn the piers of the aisles and transepts.

However, the use of this material was to reach its apotheosis in the Chapter House, completed in 1263, whose stone pillars are adorned by slender columns of Purbeck marble. And here and there, amongst the capitals of these columns, are to be found carvings of small birds and animals, nestling amongst leaves. Astonishingly, the cathedral boasts a total of 8,760 columns of Purbeck marble (one for every hour of the year), and varying in diameter from a few inches to about 18 inches.

The cathedral was completed in 1330, with the addition to its tower of a magnificent, octagonal spire. It contains the tomb of William Longspée (II), complete with an effigy of the knight in Purbeck marble. He was the son of William Longspée (I), an original benefactor of the cathedral who was present at Eastertime, 1220, when the building was dedicated to the Blessed Virgin Mary and its foundation stone laid. Longspée (II) led the English knights in the Seventh Crusade and died during the assault on Mansoura (in present-day Syria) in 1250. He was buried at Acre.

Following the carving, in 1240, of a Purbeck marble effigy of King John (died 1216) for Worcester Cathedral, the 'effigy industry' flourished. After this, no Lord or Lady, Priest or Knight, of any note, could be laid to rest without such a representation of themselves being made. Many Purbeck marble effigies were carved at Corfe; as were thousands of coffin lids, which were also in vogue.

In 1269, King Henry III, realizing the enormous value of Purbeck marble, established a group of 49 marblers and 15 marble polishers in London. He was thus able to control the sale and distribution of this commodity, which was becoming highly sought after for cathedrals and churches throughout the land – not only for columns, but also for tombs and fonts.

The origins of the 'Ancient Order of Purbeck Marblers and Stonecutters', one of the 'semi-religious Trade Guilds of medieval England' are not known. Its Chief Officer was the Warden, whose job it was to

adjust differences between the quarrymen and to order the steward, if necessary, to summon the whole body to determine a dispute.

Quarries could only be worked by a 'Freeman of the Isle of Purbeck' and to be a Freeman one had to be the legitimate son of a Freeman. This right passed to a son at the age of twenty-one – up to this time his wages belonged to his parents.

On each Shrove Tuesday, at noon, the company meets in the Town Hall at Corfe in order to conduct its business. At these Shrove Tuesday meetings, apprentices who have reached the age of twenty-one are declared 'Freemen' of the company and are considered fully qualified quarrymen although they must wait for a period of seven years before they themselves may appoint apprentices.

(Built in 1585, the aforementioned Town Hall was originally of one storey, an upper floor being added in the early eighteenth century.)

If a quarryman dies, his widow is permitted at the Shrove Tuesday meeting, to pay the sum of one shilling, thereby obtaining her 'freedom' which entitles her to take apprentices and supervise a quarry.[5]

A copy of the ancient order's 'Articles of Agreement', dated 3 March 1651, survives. In summary, the Articles were to be kept at Corfe, and used 'for

That no man of the company shall sett into his fellow tradesman's quarr [quarry] to work therein, without his consent… [Nor shall he] work partners with any man, except it be a ffreeman of the trade and the same company…

That no man of the company shall take any apprentice but that he shall keep in his own house, uprising and downlying for the term of seven years...

That no man affter he has taken his apprentice shall take any other apprentice in the whole term of seven years...

That no man in this company shall sell or make sale of any stones within the said Island [of Purbeck] unto any man but by his own proper name... [Nor shall he] undercreep [undercut] his fellow tradesman to take from him any bargin [bargain] of work of his trade...

That no man of our company shall take any apprentice that is base born [born illegitimately] or of parents that are of a loose life...

That upon any acceptance of any aprentice into the company he shall pay unto the wardens, for the use of the company, six shillings and eightpence, and one penny lofe [loaf] and two poots [pots] of beare [beer]...

That every man of our company, the Shrove Tuesday after his marriage, shall pay unto the wardens, for the use and benefitt of the company, twelfe [twelve] pence, and the last married man to bring a ffoot ball [football], according to the custom of the company.

The penalty for disobeying any of these rules was the 'forfyture [forfeiture] of five pounds'. Furthermore, it was decreed that there should be 'no noise or hindrance or disturbance to the company' at any of its 'apointed' meetings, and that no member should 'revele [reveal] or make known the secrets of the company' to any outsider.[6]

The Order had a tradition which has persisted long after the demise of the marble trade, whereby after the annual Shrove Tuesday meeting, the members of the Company would proceed to kick a football – donated by the most recently married man amongst them – from Corfe to Ower Quay (3 miles or so distant, on the southern shores of Poole Harbour). Once arrived, they would present the football, together with a pound of pepper, to the landowner as payment for the use of the right of way over his land to the Quay, from where the marble was traditionally shipped. The landowner reciprocated by presenting the quarrymen with a cake.

During the fifteenth century, the Purbeck marble industry gradually declined, and for various reasons, including

changes in architectural style... There was no longer a need for polished clustered shafts. Softer freestone lent itself more easily to sculpture and effigies.

Also, alabaster [a light-coloured translucent form of gypsum], was 'now more favoured'.[7]

Nevertheless, from time to time the marble trade underwent a brief revival, as for example when the new church at nearby Kingston in Purbeck, was built in the 1870s; or when the Temple Church in London was rebuilt after the German bombing ('Blitz') of 1941.

Continual restoration work is necessary in the numerous cathedrals viz. Exeter, Winchester, Canterbury, Chichester, Lincoln, Beverley, York and Durham, as well as in churches in which Purbeck marble is to be found. There is, therefore, an ongoing requirement for the raw material: 'a product' which is supplied, to this day, from Trelevan Haysom's quarry, and from others in the Isle of Purbeck. However, the marble is not nowadays so easily won as in medieval times – deeper digging being required to access what remains.[8]

Otherwise, the once thriving marble quarries, dotted at intervals along the length of the marble seam, are now overgrown, and their sites marked only by solitary farms.

Four
RELIGIOUS WORSHIP

St Aldhelm (circa 640 – 709), Anglo-Saxon scholar and prelate and Bishop of Sherborne, built a church in Purbeck between 690 and 700, 'two miles from the sea, near to Wareham, where Corfe Castle stands out towards the ocean'. But no trace of that building remains.[1] Subsequently, a church was built to commemorate the murder, at Corfe, of King Edward in the tenth century. It should be noted that although the late Edward is widely referred to as a saint, he was never canonized by the Pope.

The Anglo-Saxon Chronicle (compendium of Anglo-Saxon history, from the ninth to the twelfth centuries) is composed of several texts, the majority of which state that it was on the evening of 18 March 979 that the murder took place.[2] The *Vita Oswaldi* (Life of Saint Oswald, Bishop of Worcester) was written by Byrhtferth (c.970-c.1020), a priest and monk from Ramsay Abbey, Cambridgeshire (which Oswald founded). The work, which contains the earliest, and therefore, perhaps the most reliable description of the murder, 'seems to have been written about 1008, only some thirty years after the event'.[3]

One day towards evening, the illustrious and chosen king came… to the dwelling where his much-loved brother lived with the queen desiring the consolation of brotherly affection; as was becoming the chiefs and leading men, who were of the queen-mother's household, went to meet him. These, who were so depraved in heart and so befogged by the devil's own mists, that they would not have feared to lay hands on the Lord's Anointed, took evil council among themselves. Armed men were standing round him on all sides, with whom also was present a cup-bearer ready to fulfil his office. For the holy king had but few warriors with him, because he did not fear anyone, trusting in the Lord and in the strength of his own virtue. For when his betrayers encompassed him, and surrounded him, as the Jews formerly did Christ, he sat on his horse undismayed, since one delusion equal to madness was upon them all. Then the worst vileness and savage madness of the enemy Beelzebub [the devil] raged in the minds of the venomous soldiers, then arrows, poisoned with the villainy of [Pontius] Pilate [Roman prefect who presided at the trial of Jesus Christ], sped forth fiercely against the Lord and his Anointed [i.e. King Edward] who, on his father's death was chosen to preserve the kingdom and empire of a people most dear to him. The soldiers therefore detaining him, one took hold of his right hand as if he wished to salute him, another caught him roughly by the left hand at the same time wounding him. But [the king], as much as he could, cried out in a loud voice: 'Why are you breaking my right arm?' and suddenly fell from his horse and died.[4]

King Edward (circa 963 – 978) had acceded to the throne of England at the age of twelve – in 975. This was following the death of his father, the Anglo-Saxon King Edgar, known as 'the peaceful'. King Edgar's first wife and Edward's mother, was Ethelfleda whom Edgar deserted in order to marry his mistress, Elfrida. She bore him a son, Ethelred.

Dorsetshire antiquarian Thomas Bond, quoting from the Chronicle of John Brompton, the fifteenth-century Abbot of Jervaulx in Yorkshire, described what happened next.

When Elfrida heard that the king was dead she ordered his body to be conveyed to a small house hard by, that the deed which had been perpetrated might not be known. [She subsequently] commanded her servants to carry the body as speedily as possible to a secret and marshy place, where it would the least be suspected to have been buried, so that in the course of time it might be forgotten. This being done, she retired to a manor of her own, called Beer [Bere Regis], ten miles distant from Corfe.

However, the body of King Edward was subsequently discovered and conveyed by 'some devout people of Wareham' to that town's church of St Mary, where it was 'buried in a plain and homely manner on a spot where religious men afterwards built a wooden church.' However, 'Alfer, a powerful earl in Mercia, and a faithful adherent of the murdered monarch, removed the sacred body' to the Abbey of Shaftesbury, 'where it was ceremoniously re-interred'.

In the thirteenth century, during the reign of King Henry III, reference was made to 'the Chapel of St Edward at Corfe [which] was probably on the site of the present parish church, which is dedicated to King Edward the Martyr.' As for Elfrida

it is related[5] that she became extremely penitent, and abdicating her regal state, she retired to the Abbey of Wherwell, in Hampshire, which she had founded, and there, having clothed her body in hair cloth, she for many years slept at night on the ground without a pillow, and mortified her flesh with every kind of penance.[6]

To commemorate the murder of King Edward, a cross was erected in the

The Square, with plinth but no Market Cross. Photo: Bob Richards

Market Cross, and behind, Budden's butchers shop (later Holland's haberdashery, now Dragons Village Bakery). Photo: Bob Richards

Market Place: the first mention of it being in the year 1381.[7] However, in the sixteenth century it was destroyed. On St Edward's Day, 20 June 1897, a new cross was erected on the base of the former St Edward's cross, to commemorate Queen Victoria's Diamond Jubilee.

Ethelred (c. 968 – 1016) duly acceded to the English throne at the age of only ten years. During his reign the Danes invaded his kingdom.

In the thirteenth century a larger church was built on the same site, in order to accommodate not only the inhabitants of the castle, but also the multitude of townspeople who were involved in the building of it, which was an ongoing process. The first recorded rector of Corfe was Peter Doget, Cappelanus [Chaplain], who was installed in the year 1280.[8] In the fifteenth century a tower was added to the church.

Following the Dissolution of the Monasteries between 1536 and 1541 by King Henry VIII, whereby the King disbanded Catholic monasteries, priories, convents and friaries in England, Wales and Ireland, Corfe's church came under the jurisdiction of Shaftesbury Abbey, to whom it belonged. Subsequently, priests were nominated and paid for by the Lord of the Manor, who in the case of Corfe, also owned the castle.

In 1572, Queen Elizabeth I sold Corfe Castle to her favourite, the politician Sir Christopher Hatton. During his sixty-three-year tenure, Corfe was made a 'Royal Peculiar', whereby the church was granted independence from the diocese and allowed to have its own court of law. The rector, who served as 'official of this peculiar, proved wills, determined causes, and appointed surrogates'.[9]

During the English Civil War (1642-1648) much damage was done to Corfe Castle by the Parliamentarians during the siege. The Royalist periodical *Mercurius Rusticus*, stated that, for the Rebels (Parliamentarians)

> *the most advantageous part for their [gun] batteries was the church, which they without feare of prophanation used, not onely as their rampart, but their rendezvouz. Of the surplesse [surplice – white linen vestment worn over a cassock by the clergy] they made two shirts for the souldiers, they broke downe the organs, and made the pipes serve for cases to hold their powder and shot, and, not being furnished with musquet-bullets, they cut off the lead of the church [roof], and roll'd it up, and shoot it without ever casting in a mould.[10]*

It was also alleged that the Rebels stabled their horses in the church and used the font as a water trough. In 1646, compensation of £50 was paid to the church in respect of the damage suffered.[11]

In 1789, a year prior to his 1790 census of Corfe, William Morton Pitt wrote to the London Debating Society (for political, social, and democratic discussion) in regard to the creation of Sunday Schools in Purbeck and his role therein.

> *We first procured lists in every parish of the number of children it contained, above six years of age, of every [religious] persuasion; and we next*

established a sufficient number of [Sunday] schools in the different towns and villages, and in such a manner as that every child might be appointed to some school, at an inconsiderable distance from the parents' residence.

Twenty-four schools were found necessary for attaining the end proposed. They are supported by the voluntary subscriptions of the inhabitants of the several parishes....

Whilst on the one hand the schools extend religious knowledge among the ignorant, on the other they instill into the lower classes of the community, industry, decency, sobriety, and that respectful deportment towards superiors, which is perfectly consistent with true liberty and the pride of industrious independence.

Pitt considered that

six months good behaviour in the Sunday school might be considered as a qualification to be a candidate for admission to a charity school [one which is maintained by voluntary contributions and provides a full-time education].

It is not known when Corfe's Sunday School (or Schools) was founded, but in 1790, Elizabeth Flagg, a widow aged sixty-seven and living at Back [West] Street, 'knits, on parish pay' was the Sunday School's 'Mistress', and its teacher, Elizabeth Speck, aged forty-four and living at High [East] Street, wife of shoemaker Thomas, was her assistant.

Having established such Sunday Schools, Pitt declared that 'the improvement now not only in reading, but in behaviour and manners is most striking'.[12]

In 1859, Corfe's church was deemed to be in a poor state of repair. In May it was largely demolished, with the loss of several tombs and galleries, apart from the tower. It was rebuilt in 1860 in the Gothic style, the architect being T. H. Wyatt.

A few features of the former church were incorporated into the new one: amongst them, a lancet window and a thirteenth-century archway. Many monuments and memorial floor slabs in memory of minor aristocracy, gentry, clergy, and former benefactors of the church also survived. The original fourteenth-century font of Purbeck marble survived, but the reredos, also of Purbeck marble, was destroyed and replaced. However, many other monuments and tombs were allegedly destroyed in this act of Victorian 'restoration'.

The Tower
Hutchins described how the basement of the tower

has a west window of three lights over a Tudor doorway under a square label, the spandrils filled on each side with tracery and a shield. On each side of the doorway is a tabernacled niche supported by half-length sculptured figures in close-buttoned doublets with capes to their necks; that on the north side representing Wisdom in the form of a girl playing on a pipe to Folly, who is typified by a monkey.[13]

The Bells

A ring of five bells was installed in the parish church soon after the tower was built in the fifteenth century. (An additional Sanctus, or Saints bell was originally hung in the tower, but reference to this ends in 1769.) However, by 1550, only four bells were recorded. None of these original bells remain.

The present ring probably dates from the early seventeenth century, when the missing fifth bell was replaced. Hutchins described how one of the bells bore the inscription, 'Although you see I am but small, I shall be heard among you all'.[14] All the bells [apart from the treble which was added in 1790 and increased the ring to six] have been recast at least once since that date.

The rope circle at Corfe's parish church is unusual in that the bells are hung in an anti-clockwise order i.e. from treble to tenor – a circumstance that has given rise to some confusion in the past, over the numbering of the bells.[15]

The names of the founders, together with the dates on which the bells were cast, are as follows: Joshua Kipling of Portsmouth, Hampshire (1739 – two bells); Robert Wells of Aldbourne, Wiltshire (1790); Robert and James Wells of Aldbourne (1795); James Wells of Aldbourne (1804); William Dobson of Downham Market, Norfolk (1828).[16] The largest bell measured 37 inches in diameter and weighed just under half a ton.

Churchwardens accounts indicate special occasions on which the bells were rung. For example, '1675 Gave ye ringers on ye fifth of November £0-2s-6d'. These payments were made on 'Treason Day' – recalling the Gunpowder Plot of 1605.

The bells were also rung to commemorate the following events: 1685 – King James II's birthday; 1739 - the declaration of the 'War of Jenkins's Ear' against Spain; 1815 – Lord Wellington's entry into Paris, following the Battle of Waterloo.[17]

In 1991, during the incumbency of the Reverend Maurice Strike, a committee was established under the chairmanship of Tom Hunt, with the object of raising money to put the bells back into working order. They had not been rung since 1957. The outcome was, that with additional help from the Millennium Commission, sufficient funds were raised for four of the bells to be recast and retuned at the Whitechapel Foundry. Two of the bells, however, could not be recast and were therefore replaced with new ones.

The Clock
Churchwardens accounts indicate that there was a

clock in the tower as early as 1570, when Gerald Browne is mentioned as keeper of the clock. The present clock – a two-train movement… and with two external dials – was made by Thwaites & Reed of Clerkenwell in 1864.[18]

In recent times, Vernon Stockley was responsible for winding the clock, which dates from 1864. When he retired, Trish Sherwood, granddaughter of farmer Reginald Stephen Langtree, took over. It required 80 turns of the handle to wind the striker, and another 30 turns to wind the clock itself, she said. Finally, in the 1950s, it was electrified.

The Rectory
The traditional rectory for Corfe was Glebe House, situated a mile, or so, from the village on the road to Church Knowle, close to the parish boundary. According to Hutchins

the Parsonage house was destroyed in the Civil Wars, and part of the ruins were brought away to repair the church damaged in the siege. It has since been rebuilt, and stands detached about one mile from the town and situated upon an eminence to the south-west of the castle, in a very pleasant situation, commanding a beautiful, picturesque view of that fine ruin.[19]

In fact, the property was rebuilt in the late seventeenth century, during the rectorship of the Reverend Nicholas Gibbon (1644 to 1697).[20]

The rectory was 'greatly improved' by Sir Thomas Bankes l'Anson, Rector of Corfe from 1748 to 1799 and a kinsman of the Bankes family. It was further modified by his successor William Bond, rector 1800-1820. With its farm and 59 acres of land, this would have provided the incumbent with a comfortable living. The Reverend William J. de Kilpeck was the rector from 1899 to 1938. Having no transport of his own, that reverend gentleman was obliged to hire a taxi from Mr Ernest Sheasby to convey him to the village, or to the railway station.

Ada Cooper (née Fooks born in 1912) lived at Corfe from the age of ten. In the 1920s, as she recalled, the Reverend William de Kilpeck's curate was the Reverend Singleton, who occupied the curatage in East Street, and when he left the village, Ethel Dru Drury, the doctor's wife, stepped in and offered her assistance. The rector retired in 1938 at the age of ninety.

Ada recalled how, at church on Sundays, the villagers occupied 'free sittings' in the south aisle, whereas the central aisle was reserved for those people who paid a 'pew rent' and whose names appeared on printed cards on their pews. The organist was Billy Moss. 'A young lad who did his best', he was the son of Robert, the blacksmith. Mr George, partially shielded by a curtain, 'blew the bellows' i.e. worked the pump which blew air through the organ pipes when the organist was playing. When Billy was called up for the First World War, Billy Burt, 'another lad', took his place, but 'he stammered a lot, and it was difficult to follow at times'.

The bells were rung by a team of bell-ringers at morning and evening service, said Ada, and the curfew (time after which people were required to remain indoors) was rung at 8 p.m. during the winter months, to indicate the time of day. When a person died the bell was tolled once for a child; twice for a woman; and three times for a man, followed by a number of chimes corresponding to the age of the deceased. Thus the villagers could usually guess for whom the bell tolled.

The last incumbent of Glebe House was the Reverend William Yorke Batley, who succeeded the Reverend de Kilpeck in 1938 and held the living until 1948. This, of course, included the years of the Second World War. The new rector, said Ada Cooper, considered that Glebe House was too far distant from Corfe, so he purchased the head gardener's cottage belonging to Mortons House; added a new east wing, and this became the rectory. When the Reverend Batley retired his wife Frances, founded Corfe's branch of the Mothers Union and also the Women's Institute.

Batley was succeeded by Canon Lancelot Farquharson Addison (1948-1955) who, said Editha Langtree (born at Corfe in 1882), 'was a very nice, kindly gentlemen'.[21]

In the early 1940s, various alterations were made to the church including the addition of two new windows and the replacement of the Victorian tiled floor by stone.[22] Addison was succeeded by the Reverend Roger de Beaufort Welchman (rector from 1955-1974).

Benjamin Thomas ('Tom') C. Cattle was born at Norden in 1906 and lived at Corfe from the age of five. He was not impressed by the manner in which the inside of the church had been 'torn out'. He particularly regretted the removal of the choir stalls. In former times he said, 'We had such a large choir. They were such grand times'.[23]

For twenty-five years, during the first half of the twentieth century, Dr Dru Drury served as churchwarden of the parish church, where he kept the churchyard tidy and cut the grass.

Nonconformist worship in Corfe

Members of Protestant Churches which dissented from the established Church of England, were traditionally known as 'Dissenters', and later as

'Nonconformists'. In England, it was not until the passing of the Toleration Act of 1689, that such people were allowed the right of religious assembly and permitted to worship freely in premises licensed by Anglican bishops.

Congregationalism

Congregationalism (or Presbyterianism – the two being synonymous), is a system of organization among Christian churches whereby individual churches are largely self-governing.[24]

In the latter half of the eighteenth century, at Corfe, the following premises were licenced as places of worship, where Nonconformist services were permitted to be held: the dwelling house of John Farrell (Farwell), labourer and hardware man of Back (West) Street, Presbyterian, 26 April 1770; the house at the rear of two dwelling houses in West Street (a complex with courtyard, subsequently known as Well Court) occupied by John Roe, shoemaker, and William Nounan, Presbyterians, 4 October 1774.[25] (Presbyterian – Protestant Church or denomination governed by elders all of equal rank.[26])

Notable Nonconformist families in Corfe were Havilland, Stockley, Butler, George, and Smith.

In 1810, Thomas Denny became Corfe's first, regular, ordained Nonconformist minister, who 'labored earnestly in the town and neighbouring villages', until the year 1813.[27]

On 18 January 1815 in the rear garden of Well Court, a newly-built Congregational chapel was opened for Nonconformists, complete with gallery and 'capable of holding 200 or 300 persons'. A Sunday School was also established.[28] The Reverend Mr Shickle of Hoxton Academy, Middlesex, for the education of Dissenters, was the chapel's first minister. However,

the young pastor, who had raised such high expectations, was smitten down with brain fever, and died September 8th, aged thirty-three.

In that year of 1815 it was reported that 'attendance at chapel was good during the day, and at night crowded'.

The minister from 1827 was George Hubbard, who lived at the manse (house provided for the minister), formerly an inn called The Swan, on the corner of Sandy Hill Lane. In 1835 a new Congregational chapel was built in East Street, to which minister Hubbard transferred. Previously, on this site, had stood a barn. This had been used by Corfe's Quakers (members of the Religious Society of Friends – a Christian movement devoted to peaceful principles and rejecting both formal ministry and all set forms of worship[29]) as a meeting house, and the garden as their burial plot.[30]

Above: *Well Court, West Street: the chapel.*

Right: *Well Court, West Street: steps from which John Wesley preached in 1774.*

Below: *Reverend George Hubbard, Congregational Minister, Corfe Castle, 1827-1874.* Photo: Corfe Castle Evangelical Congregational Church.

In the earlier years of Mr Hubbard's ministry, he was viewed with distrust and dislike by the local gentry, and even the class whom he specially sought to serve, failed to see in him a friend. Indeed, at a time of political excitement, the prejudice against him was so strong that his effigy was burnt in the streets.

The phrase 'political excitement' referred to the fact that, particularly in rural areas and in mining communities, Nonconformists who were anxious to improve their civic status and also to bring about the dismantling of the established church, were associated with political radicalization.[31]

With a brave heart, he plodded on, keeping a cheerful temper, returning good for evil, ever ready with a kind word and a helping hand. So, long before the end, all opposition had been lived down, and the respect and affection of all parties had been won. He died peacefully in 1870, at the ripe age of 90.[32]

The chapel continues today as the Evangelical Congregational Church.

Congregational Chapel and two of its former ministers. Original by William Churchill, Wareham. Photo: Bob Richards.

Methodism

Methodism, a Christian, Protestant denomination, was founded in 1739 by John Wesley (1703-1791), priest and lecturer in Greek at Oxford University. How did Methodism come to Corfe?

In October 1774, Mary Burt of Swanage walked from her home town to Salisbury (a distance of almost 50 miles), carrying her baby and in company with two other women named Webber and Collins, in order to meet John Wesley and persuade him to visit Purbeck and preach there.[33] She was evidently successful, because on the evening of 11 October, said he, at Corfe

> *I preached in a meadow near the town, to a deeply attentive congregation gathered from all parts of the island.[34]*

In September 1776, Wesley paid a second visit to Corfe where, said he, on the 5th

> *At six (a.m.) I preached in the yard adjoining to the preaching house. It was a season both of conviction and consolation.[35]*

It is traditionally believed that it was at Well Court in East Street that Wesley preached on that occasion. At the time, the property was owned by the Havilland (or 'Havelland') family. (It was here, in the rear garden, that the Congregationalists would build their aforementioned chapel, almost forty years later.)

We do not know how the society progressed numerically, but there is evidence that a building or dwelling house in the tenure or occupation of George Speck was used for Methodist worship.[36]

A Methodist preacher was not attached to one chapel in particular. Instead, he or she visited various chapels on 'the circuit'. Chapels also had their own local 'lay' preachers. At the time of Wesley's second visit to Corfe in 1776, Salisbury in Wiltshire was the headquarters of the Methodist Circuit, of which Purbeck was a part.

Primitive Methodism was a major offshoot of Methodism, whose adherents were members of a society of Methodists which was formed in 1811, two decades after Wesley's death. Furthermore, the Circuits of Primitive Methodists were separate from those of Wesleyan Methodists. Since about 1839, religious services were held by members in Corfe, and up until 1876 at least, Primitive Methodists continued to meet 'in a house in the village'.[37]

In 1859, Corfe's first Wesleyan (following the teachings of John Wesley, and the main branch of Methodism which he founded[38]) chapel was built, behind a row of terraced cottages on the west side of East Street, abutting onto The Halves.

In spring 1871, the Wesleyan Methodist Circuit was divided into smaller areas, and Swanage became headquarters of the circuit that included Corfe.

As Sunday School work developed and more space was needed, the Society under the leadership of the Rev. T. Ivens (Supt.) and the Society Steward Mr George Ford [farmer, of Bucknowle House] decided to build a new church.

Corfe's Methodist chapel was duly built in East Street and opened on 21 September 1905.[39] Many private individuals and organization Contributed towards the costs, including the Sunday Schools of Swanage and Langton Matravers, as plaques on the exterior wall testify. Two of the wall plaques bear the following inscriptions: 'In memory of John Bolson, converted under Wesley 1774'; 'In memory of Stephen Paine preached thirty-eight years'.

In 1932, several of the larger Methodist denominations came together with the foundation of the Methodist Union.

In the year 2000, Corfe's Methodist chapel was closed. It was sold in 2001 and converted into residential accommodation.[40]

Five

CORFE AND THE ELIZABETHAN PIRATES

When Queen Elizabeth I came to the throne in 1558, she found herself under pressure from France, Spain, and Scotland (whose merchantmen were under constant threat of attack by English pirates) to suppress piracy.

Seven years later, in 1565, commissioners were appointed and charged with apprehending the pirates; examining them before a jury of twelve men, and if appropriate, sending them for trial at the Admiralty Sessions. The weakness of this system was that the commissioners were chosen from local justices and deputy lieutenants, who themselves had a vested interest in piracy.

In 1576, the Queen appointed Sir Christopher Hatton (one of her favourite courtiers), Constable of Corfe Castle, Lord Lieutenant of the Isle of Purbeck, and also its Vice Admiral. Her Majesty also appointed Hatton as Guardian of Brownsea Island, which is strategically situated at the mouth of Poole Harbour. Hatton, however, rarely visited Purbeck: his family seat being Holdenby in Northamptonshire.

Hatton's deputy was Francis Hawley, a person of modest means who did reside at Corfe Castle, 'with a garrison of impoverished Purbeck gentry under his command'.[1]

In 1577, when a 'Commission for the Reformation of Piracy' was established, the commissioners came under powerful scrutiny from officials of the High Court of the Admiralty. This commission reported back to the Privy Council – a committee of the Queen's closest advisers – to which it was answerable.

In 1578, several Dorset pirates were apprehended at sea. Of these, seven were tried, condemned to death, and hanged at Wapping on the banks of the River Thames. Following this setback, the remaining pirates were obliged to shift the centre of their activities from West Lulworth and Weymouth to Studland in the Isle of Purbeck.

The village of Studland, which was central to the pirates' operations, lies between South Haven Point and the entrance to Poole Harbour to the north, and Handfast Point and its pinnacle rocks – known as 'The Old Harry Rocks' – to the south.

Why did the pirates find Studland such an attractive location? There were several reasons. They were undoubtedly aware that Hatton, who was sympathetic to their cause, was the Queen's favourite, and therefore 'could not be touched';[2] and Purbeck was entirely under Hatton's jurisdiction. They could also rely on the cooperation of Francis Hawley. Poole Harbour, which was only a short distance away, provided safe anchorage in all weathers, whereas Studland Bay was exposed to the westerly gales. Also, it was easier for the pirates to re-victual their ships within Poole Harbour, whereas in Studland Bay they were obliged to lie at anchor offshore, there being no natural place for their ships to dock.

Hawley's officer/servant at Studland was George Fox of Wareham, whose duty it was to board all pirated ships – 'prizes' - which entered Studland Bay and make an inventory of their contents in order to calculate what customs duty was payable; also to claim his share of those goods on behalf of Hatton, his master.[3]

The principal pirates operating out of Studland Bay in the latter part of the sixteenth century were Clinton Atkinson, William Valentine (alias Vaughan), William Arnewood, Thomas Walton (alias Purser,) and John Piers. Their leader was the infamous Stephen Heynes, who once placed a knotted rope around the head of the master of a captured vessel and used it as a tourniquet in order to extract information from him. The pirate chiefs came from such places as London, Cornwall, and elsewhere. None were local men.

The pirates' ill-gotten gains were sold to merchants who came from Poole, and from as far afield as Hampshire and the Isle of Wight. The great barn in Studland village served as a repository for pirated goods.

When they were not at sea, the pirates spent their leisure time drinking and playing dice and cards in the inns in Studland at which they lodged. There were three such inns. They belonged to Roger Munday, who was also a member of Heynes's ship's company; to his brother William, who was also a fisherman, and to Joan Chaddocks of Corfe.

Piracy was a brutal business, both on sea and on land, as this statement by pirate Clinton Atkinson reveals: 'William Munday, his house [inn] is the hell of the world, and he the devil.'[4] One may imagine the pirates, strutting about in fine clothes of satin, velvet and lace, which they had pirated; arguing over games of cards and dice, and engaging in drunken brawls with one another.

Even in Studland, remote though it was, the pirates were not beyond the reach of the authorities. This, William Munday discovered in February 1581, when he was summoned to London on suspicion of being implicated in piracy, and examined by Dr David Lewis, Judge of Her Majesty's High Court of Admiralty.

In his statement to the court, Munday admitted that his wife had received a quantity of flax from the Studland pirates, 'whiche she delyvered to Francys Clerke [presumably meaning Francis Hawley's clerk].' He also stated that Hawley had sent some of the pirated wine which he had seized, to the City of London. Munday also admitted that he had been in the company of the pirates mentioned in the article, 'on lande, and hath eate and drinke with them,' but he 'could not neither durst apprehend them'.

Munday also admitted that his brother Roger, had obtained a 'pipe [cask] of Canarye wynes [sweet wines from the Canary Islands]' from the pirates, which he sold at his inn, 'whereof this examinante [Munday] and others drancke.'

Munday stated that the previous July (1580), when he was out fishing in his boat, he was summoned by Captain Arnewood who had brought a captured French ship into the bay laden with 'fish of the bancke' (a reference to the Grand Bank fishing grounds of Newfoundland.) Whereupon, Arnewood unloaded 'thre hundrethe [hundredweight] or upwards of fish for George Foxe' who was aboard Arnewood's man-of-war at the time. Munday then took the fish ashore, where his son Thomas, delivered it to Fox. It was then taken by Francis Hawley. For his trouble, Munday was rewarded with, 'thre cople [six] of fishe' by Arnewood.

Munday also stated that George Fox and one of the pirates came aboard Arnewood's ship, from which Fox carried away 'thre or foure suger [sugar] loaves.' Munday also said that Thomas Aires [Ayres, one of Hawley's deputies at Corfe Castle] 'had 2 pipes of Canarye wynes' which were unshipped and taken to his farm barn. In the event, Munday was released without charge. Others were not so fortunate.[5]

In October 1581, Studland pirate John Piers, was betrayed when he was apprehended by fellow pirate, Thomas Walsh. Piers and several of his companions were tried at Corfe Castle, found guilty, and condemned. In March 1582 they were hanged at Studland Beach in the traditional manner: so that, as the tide came in, their corpses appeared to dance upon the waves. Meanwhile, when the remaining pirates failed to take the hint and cease their nefarious activities, it was inevitable that further setbacks would follow.

In 1583, four ships, whose task it was to pursue pirates, were fitted out by the Crown. That summer, the Queen's ships *Bark Talbot* and *Unicorn* captured seven of the pirates' men-of-war, together with three prizes, which the pirates had captured. The outcome was that 43 pirates were examined in the Tower of London by Dr Julius Caesar, Judge of the High Court of Admiralty, together with three others.

At the examination it transpired that when the ship *Anne* from the Port of London was captured by pirate Stephen Haynes and brought into Studland Bay, her cargo of wax was sold, and George Fox 'bought the cottons for the Dorchester merchants'.[6]

Furthermore, when Hawley's servant William King, was sailing in a small boat in Studland Bay and was summoned aboard a pirate ship, whom should he discover there but John Uvedale of Uvedale House (otherwise known as the Manor House) Corfe, who in that year of 1583 had been appointed mayor of the village, together with Wareham merchant, Thomas Perkins. Clearly, a business deal was being conducted.[7]

On another occasion, Stephen Haynes captured a ship the cargo of which included monkeys and parrots. These, he brought into Studland Bay, whereupon John Uvedale 'carried a pair of birds to Corfe'.[8]

Finally, Francis Hawley received from William Valentine a pirated gilt rapier and a Holy Bible,[9] and from Clinton Atkinson, both Hawley and Uvedale received pirated timber.[10]

The prisoners were all found guilty, but only seven of them, all captains, were condemned to death; the remainder being pardoned. Those hanged at Wapping included Atkinson, Purser, and Vaughan. (Steven Heynes escaped the hangman's noose, having been swept overboard in a storm and drowned the year previously.)[11]

Three weeks after the hangings, Uvedale and Ayres led a band of Purbeck islanders in an attack on Corfe Castle, with a view to avenging the deaths of the pirates. They stole the castle's lead and glass, and Uvedale used its stones to build a new house.[12]

In the autumn of 1583, another 19 people from Purbeck were summoned to London to be examined. They included the Munday brothers; George Fox; Francis Hawley; Hawley's deputy John Uvedale, of Corfe; Thomas Ayres, and William Munday. In the light of his support for the pirates, Hawley was demoted from Vice Admiral of Purbeck to Deputy Vice Admiral. Soon afterwards, however, he obtained the post of Deputy Vice Admiral of Dorset.

For Munday, this was to be his second examination and again, it was Dr Lewis who undertook it. This time, it was in respect of 'Articles [article – clause or paragraph of a legal document] given against him' on behalf of Peter Bard, Arnold Duverger, and other merchants of Rochelle (La Rochelle – a French sea port on the bay of Biscay,) where it was alleged that, 'certayne spoyles [had been] committed bye Clinton Atkinson on their goods.'

Munday confirmed that Atkinson and his company had, the previous June, brought two captured French ships into Studland Bay, which were laden 'with Flaunders commodities of all sortes' (Flanders formerly being a region of north-west Europe) which they 'made sale of.' Munday also stated that he was commanded by Hawley to accompany him to Atkinson's ship 'in Studlande Roade' (a 'road' being a safe anchorage) to see who was coming in their boats to buy and carry away 'those goodes whiche he had.'

On that occasion, said Munday, Hawley was presented with three sugar loaves, one or two Spanish 'skynnes', and two pipes of wines with sugar.[13]

A 'skynne' was the hide of a bull out of which shoes – and in particular ladies' shoes – were made. The hides were, therefore, highly sought after. They originated from Córdoba in Spain, where they were a product of the bull-fighting industry.

All of the accused, however, appear to have escaped relatively unscathed. But piracy in Studland now came to an end. Nevertheless, the Munday family, and doubtless the families of all the other former pirates, continued to live and multiply: the children of William's son Thomas, all being christened in Studland's church of St Nicholas.

Six
CORFE CASTLE AND THE BANKES FAMILY

A most dramatic episode in the history of Corfe Castle occurred during the English Civil War of 1642 - 1648, when the castle was in the possession of Sir John Bankes and his wife Mary. This was when the castle came under siege, from May to August 1643, and again between January and February 1646.

Bankes was born in Keswick in Cumberland in 1589. His father was John, a merchant, who subsequently became a minister of religion, and his mother was Jane, née Malton. His family's wealth was derived from graphite mines which it owned in the county: the 'lead' being used in the manufacture of pencils. In 1614 he was called to the bar.

In 1616, Bankes, now a successful lawyer, married Mary Hawtrey (born in 1603) from Ruislip in Middlesex. Mary's father Ralph Hawtrey, Esquire, was of Norman descent. Mary's mother was also Mary, née Altham. Bankes and his wife Mary, would have a total of three sons and six daughters.

In 1624, Bankes became Member of Parliament for Wootton Bassett in Wiltshire. In 1631 he was knighted. In 1634 he was appointed attorney general, at a salary of approximately £10,000 per year.

Mary, Lady Bankes: enamel miniature by Henry Pierce Bone.
Photo: the National Trust

In 1635, Bankes purchased Corfe Castle and its landed estate, from Lady Elizabeth, estranged widow of the late Lord Chief Justice Sir Edward Coke, who had died in the previous year. With the purchase came the title of Lieutenant of the Isle of Purbeck and Constable of Corfe Castle. He furnished the castle with the finest furniture, imported from France. His library contained a magnificent collection of leather-bound books embossed with gold leaf. In 1636, the Bankes's oldest son John died, unmarried, whereupon his younger brother Ralph, became heir.

In January 1641, Bankes was appointed Chief Justice at the Court of Common Pleas – a division of the King's Court which had jurisdiction over civil matters. He also presided, during the summer months, over the assizes on the Western Circuit (district in which a judge hears court cases).

In respect of the current dispute between Charles and Parliament Bankes wrote, as follows, on 21 May 1642 to Mr G. Green, Member of Parliament for Corfe

> *I have studied all meanes, which way matters may be brought to a good conclusion between the King and the housses [of Parliament], all high wayes and ways of force will be distructive; and if we should have civill warrs, it would make us a miserable people, and might introduce foreign powers; therefore, there is no other way left but the way of accommodation...*[1]

Clearly, Bankes was not a warmonger. In December 1642, he received an honorary degree of Doctor of Civil Law.

The origins of the English Civil War, of which the besiegement of Corfe Castle was a part, lay in the autocratic behaviour of the monarch, King Charles I. Charles came to the throne on 27 March 1625. On 13 June he married Princess Henrietta Maria, daughter of King Henry IV of France. The new queen was a Catholic, which made the marriage unpopular.

In 1628, Parliament presented Charles with the 'Petition of Right', which sought to establish rights for the king's subjects on matters of taxation, property, and *habeas corpus*. This, he reluctantly accepted. However, the following year he dissolved Parliament, and for the next eleven years, until 1640, he ruled without it. During this time, he condoned the persecution of the Puritans (those who believed that the Church of England needed to be reformed.) He also raised taxes by devious and illegal means.

In 1637, Charles attempted to impose a new prayer book on the Scots, who responded by signing the National Covenant in an attempt to preserve their religious identity. In 1641 he abolished the Star Chamber – a court of law established in 1487 whose function was, purportedly, to hear individual petitions to the King. In fact, it became synonymous with the abuse of power by the monarch and his circle.

At Eastertime 1641, Bankes was summoned to York, to join the King. He was now appointed to the Privy Council – the King's advisory body. Mindful of the need for security, Bankes promptly moved his wife and family to Corfe Castle, taking care to stock up with a plentiful supply of food and ammunition. Perhaps he had foreseen that trouble was brewing, and this is why he had acquired the castle in the first place. As for their two eldest daughters, Mary and Alice, they were already married and lived in Oxford and Buckinghamshire respectively. Meanwhile, the youngest daughter Arabella, was a mere infant.

In 1642, Charles attempted, unsuccessfully, to arrest 5 Members of Parliament. When the King was forced to flee from London in January 1642, he established his royal capital at Oxford, and made his home at Christchurch College. On 22 August he raised his Royal Standard at Nottingham. It bore the legend, 'Give Unto Caesar His Due'. This marked the commencement of the English Civil War. A week later, Huntingdonshire farmer and Parliamentarian Oliver Cromwell, mustered a troop of cavalry – 'Ironsides' – to fight against the King.

An account of events leading up to the siege of Corfe Castle – May to August 1643 – was given in the contemporary Royalist publication, *Mercurius Rusticus*. As expected, it is heavily biased in favour of the King, and highly contemptuous of the Rebels.

The account begins by describing just how formidable a fortification Corfe Castle was.

> *The structure of the castle is so strong, the ascent so steep, the Walls so massi[v]e and thick, that it is one of the impregnablest forts of the kingdome, and of very great concernment, in respect of its command over the island [of Purbeck] and the places about it.*

In Dorsetshire, the Royalists suffered many setbacks as the Parliamentarians – 'Rebels' – took over most of the county.

By May 1643, *Mercurius Rusticus* reported that

> *the rebels, under the command of Sir Walter Earle [Erle], Sir Thomas Trenchard, and others, had possessed themselves of Dorchester, Lyme [Regis], Melcome [Regis], Weymouth, War[e]ham, and Poole (Portland Castle being treacherously delivered to the Rebels).*

Finally, only Corfe Castle remained

> *in obedience to the King; but the rebels, knowing how much it concerned them to adde this castle to their other garrisons, to make all the sea-coast wholly for them, and thinking it more feizable to gain it by treachery than open hostility, resolved to lay hold on an opportunity comming [sic] on, to see if they could become masters of it.*

The Rebels first attempted to ambush the Royalists, but their attempt failed, as is now explained.

> *There is an ancient usage [already mentioned] that the mayor and barons (as they call them) of Corffe Castle, accompanied by the gentry of the island, have permission from the lord of the castle on May-Day to course a stagge, which every year is performed with much solemnity and great concourse of*

people. On this day some troopes of horse from Dorchester and other places came into the island, intending to find other game than to hunt the stagge, their business being suddenly to surprise the gentlemen in the hunting and to take the castle; the newes of their comming disperst the hunters, and spoyled the sport for that day, and made the Lady Bank[e]s to give order for the safe custodie of the castle gates, and to keep them shut against all commers.

The troopers having mist [missed] their prey on the hills, (the gentlemen having withdrawne themselves) some of them came to the castle under a pretence to see it, but entrance being denyed them, the common soldiers used threatning language, casting out words implying some intentions to take the castle, but the commanders (who better knew how to conceale their resolu-tions) utterly disavowed any such thought, denying that they had such commission; however the Lady Banks very wisely, and like her selfe, hence tooke occasion to call in a guard to assist her, not knowing how soone she might have occasion to make use of them, it being now more than probable that the rebels had a designe upon the castle. The taking in [of] this guard, as it secured her at home, so it rendred her suspected abroad; from thence forward there was a watchfull and vigilant eye to survey all her actions; whatsoever she sends out, or sends for in, is suspected; her ordinary provisions for her family are by some multiplyed, and reported to be more than double what indeed they were, as if she had now an intention to victuall and man the castle against the forces of the two Houses of Parliament.

The Rebels tried to force Lady Bankes to surrender to them the most powerful weapons in her armoury – her four small cannon – but she refused, and instead

dispatched messengers to Dorchester and Poole, to entreat the commis-sioners that the small peeces might remain in the castle for her own defence.

[Whereupon] a promise was made, that they should be left to her posses-sion. But there passed not many dayes before forty seamen (they in the castle not suspecting any such thing) came very early in the morning to demand the peeces; the Lady in person (early as it was) goes to the gates and desires to see their warrant; they produce one, under the hands of some of the commis-sioners; but, instead of delivering them [surrendering the cannon], though at that time there were but five men in the castle, yet these five, assisted by the maid-servants at their Ladies command, mount these peeces on their carriages again, and l[o]ading one of them, they gave fire, which small thunder so affrighted the sea-men that they all quitted the place and ran away. They being gone, by beat of drumme, she summons helpe into the castle, and,

upon the alarme given, a very considerable guard of tenants and friends came to her assistance, there being withall some fifty armes brought into the castle, from severall parts of the island; this guard was kept in the castle about a weeke…

The Rebels now sent threatening letters to Lady Bankes, who finally agreed to surrender her four cannon in return for being left in peace. Nevertheless, 'this wise lady knew too well to rest satisfied or secured in these promises'. She therefore prepared for a siege, furnishing the castle with

provisions of all sorts [including] an hundrede and halfe of [gun] powder, and a quantity of match [wick or cord designed to burn at a uniform rate, for firing a cannon] proportionable.

When she heard that friendly forces were in the area, namely Prince Maurice (of the Palatinate – territory of the German Empire ruled by the count palatine of the Rhine), and the Marquess Hertford (later 2nd Duke of Somerset), Lady Bankes appealed to them for help.

She, by her messenger made her addresse to them… desiring their assistance, and in particular that they would be pleased to take into their

serious consideration to send some commanders thither, to take the charge of the castle; hereupon they send Captaine Laurence [or 'Lawrence'], sonne of Sir Edward Laurence, a gentleman of that island [of Purbeck], to command in chief; but he, comming without a commission, could not command moneyes or provisions to be brought in untill it was too late.[2]

Corfe Castle: the Model Village.
Photo: Ed Paris

Seven

THE SIEGE

The first principal siege of Corfe Castle began in the summer of 1643 and was led by Sir Walter Erle of Charborough in South Dorsetshire; but Lady Bankes held fast. The following account, given in *Mercurius Rusticus*, was highly biased in favour of the Royalists.

The first time the rebells faced the castle they brought a body of between two and three hundred horse and foot, and two peeces of ordnance, and from the hil[l]s played on the castle, fired [set fire to] foure houses in the town, and then summoned [demanded the surrender of] the castle; but receiving a deniall, for that time, they left it. But on the three and twentieth of June, the sagacious knight, Sir Walter Earle (that hath the gift of discerning treasons, and might have made up his nine and thirty treasons [to] forty, by reckoning in his own), accompanied by Captaine [William] Sidenham [Sydenham, of Wynford Eagle], Captaine Henry Jarvis, Captaine Skut, sonne [son] of that arch-traytor Skut [George Skut, MP] of Poole, with a body of betweene five and six hundred, came and possessed themselves of the towne [of Corfe], taking the opportunity of a misty morning, that they might find no resistance from the castle.

They brought with them to the siege a demy-canon, a culverin [long-barrelled cannon] and two sacres [sakers – medium-sized cannon]; with these and their small shot, they play[e]d on the castle on all quarters of it, with good observation of advantages, making their battery strongest where they thought the castle weakest. And to bind the souldiers by tye [tie] of conscience to an eager prosecution of the siege, they administer them an oath, and mutually binde themselves to most unchristian resolutions, that if they found the defendants obstinate not to yield, they would maintain the siege to victory, and then deny quarter unto all, killing without mercy, men, women and children.

As to bring on [encourage] their own souldiers they abused them with falshoods, telling them that the castle stood in a levell [i.e. on flat ground], yet with good advantages of approach, that there were but forty men in the castle, whereof twenty were for them; that there was rich booty, and the like: so during the seige [sic] they used all base, unworthy meanes, to corrupt the defendants to betray the castle into their hand; the better sort they endeavor to corrupt with bribes, to the rest they offer double pay, and the whole plunder of the castle…

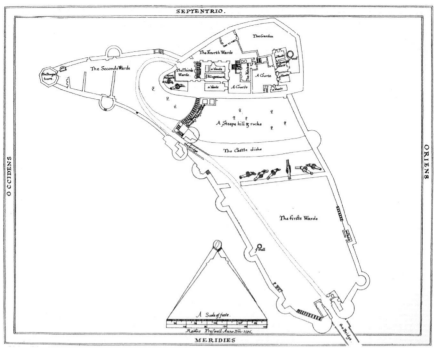

Plan of Corfe Castle, from drawing by Ralph Treswell 1586.

In an attempt to undermine the walls, the Rebels now brought two siege engines into play: the 'sowe' and the 'boar'.

> *The great sow was 35 foote long and 9 foote broade: it was made upon 4 wheeles, made of whole timbers, bound aboutt with hoopes of iron; their axell trees were one, the rim was great round bars of iron, the beams she was bu[i]lt upon being of timbar [timber]. Thaie [they] had cros[s] beams within to worck with there [their] levars [levers], to forse [force] her along as thaie ple[a]sed to guide har. The hinder part of the sow was left open for there [their] men to goe in and outt att. The fore parte of the sow had 4 dowres [doors], 2 in the ruffe [roof] and 2 one [?in] the lower parte, which did hang upon great iron huckes [hooks], but were not open till they came to the wall of the castell [castle], when thaie intended to worck through the castell [walls] with there [their] tooles thaie [they] had provided... The sow was lickwaies [likewise], covard [covered] ovar with 2 rowes of hides and 2 rowes of sheepe skinnes: soe that noe musket bullet or steele arow [arrow] could pearse [pierce] it, of which triell [attempt] was often made.*
>
> *The lesar [lesser] sow was made only to goe before, to cleere the waie [way],*

52

being but 6 foote longe and 3 foote brod [broad], bult strong, as above, only run upon one whele [wheel] lick [like] a wheele barow, and cheefely employd to goe for vitell [provisions] for the great sow to the camp, and for any to com to the bigg sow when thaie desired.[1]

However, because of the skill of the defenders at firing their muskets at the unprotected legs of the occupants of the siege engines, the attack failed.

Mercurius Rusticus made the following sarcastic comments about the behaviour of Sir Walter Erle and the Rebels.

As prodigall as they were of the blood of their common souldiers, they were sparing enough of their owne; it was a generall observation, that valiant Sir Walter never willingly exposed himself to any hazard, for, being by chance endangered by a bullet, shot through his coat, afterwards he put on a beares skinne, and to the eternal honour of this knight's valour, be it recorded, for feare of musquet-shot he was seen to creep on all foure [foures], on the sides of the hill, to keep himselfe out of danger.

The base cowardisme in the assaylants, added courage and resolution to the defendants; therefore, not compell'd by want, but rather to brave the rebels, they sallyed out, and brought in eight cowes and a bull into the castle, without the losse of a man, or a man wounded. At another time, five boyes fetcht in foure cowes.

The Rebels having made no progress whatsoever, the Earl of Warwick now sent 150 mariners, and

severall cart-loads of petars [petard – a small bomb], granadoes [grenades], and other warlike provision, with scaling ladders to assault the castle.

However, when the Rebel commanders found that even by bribery, they could not persuade 'such abject, low-spirited man' to attack, they decided to

resolve on another course, which was to make them drunke, knowing that drunkennesse makes some men fight like lyons [lions], that being sober would runne away like hares.

The Rebels now stormed the castle on all sides, whereupon the 'valiant Captain Laurence and the greater part of the souldiers' defended the 'middle ward' – presumably the south-west bailey – whilst Lady Bankes, 'to her eternall honour be it spoken) with her daughters, women, and five souldiers', defended the 'upper ward' – presumably the inner bailey.

*and did bravely performe what she undertooke; for by heaving over stones
and hot embers, they repelled the rebels and kept them from climbing their
ladders, thence to throw in that wild-fire [burning embers or pitch], which
every rebell had ready in his hand.*

The Rebels finally abandoned the siege, and Sir Walter handed over
command to Captain Sydenham who, with his men

*kept sanctuary in the church till night, meaning to suppe, and run away
by starre-light; but supper being ready, and set on the table, an alarme was
given that the King's forces were coming: this newes took away Sydenham's
stomack… he leaves his artillery, ammunition, and (which with these men
was a something) a good supper, and ran away to take boat for Poole; leaving
likewise at the shore about an hundred horse, to the next takers, which next
day proved good prize to the souldiers of the castle.[2]*

Thus, on 4 August 1643, the first major siege of Corfe Castle, which had
lasted for six weeks, ended. But this would not be the last. George Bankes now
takes up the story.

Because Lady Bankes's husband, Sir John, had 'denounced the Earl of Essex,
Lord Manchester and others, as guilty of high treason for continuing in arms
against the King', and because of his own continuing support for the monarch,
Parliament decreed that he a), should forfeit all his property and b), be
denounced as 'a traitor to the state'.[3]

In autumn 1643, Bankes paid what was to be his last visit to his home at
Corfe Castle – an occasion on which his youngest child William, was conceived.
The child was born at Corfe Castle in June 1644. Alas, he was destined never
to meet his father. Here at Corfe, Sir John found the castle battered, but intact.
However, the church had been desecrated and stripped of its roof. As for the
shops, they had been plundered, and the cottages in the vicinity burned.

*The poor families thus expelled found their refuge within the walls which
they had so faithfully helped to defend. There was much to render this a joyful
meeting at Corfe Castle, for it seemed as if the sun of the King's fortunes,
arrested in its decline, stood still in the west, with a brilliant lustre that gave
hope of a better morrow.[4]*

In January 1644 the King assembled his own Royalist parliament in Oxford:
the first session of which commenced on the 22nd of that month in the Great Hall
of Christchurch College. In attendance were 82 peers (i.e. the majority of the
House of Lords), and 175 commoners (i.e. about 1/3 of the membership of the

House of Commons). However, continued George Bankes, in that year of 1644

the tide of the royal success, which had flowed so steadily through the western counties in the preceding year, was now ebbing fast in the county of Dorset. Corfe Castle was almost the only place of strength between Exeter and London which still held out for the royal cause.[5]

In February 1644, Bankes's London home was sequestered by Parliament and sold. And now, to add to Lady Bankes's misfortunes, on 28 December her husband died in Oxford after a short illness, at the home of his son-in-law Sir Robert Jenkinson, with whom he had been staying. Surprisingly, Lady Bankes and her family were able to make the journey to that city for the funeral. Did the Rebels allow her safe passage, or did she receive a Royalist escort? Whichever was the case is not known. Bankes was buried at the city's Christchurch Cathedral and a memorial erected to his memory.

Following her husband's death, Lady Bankes and her children

were declared malignants [malicious contrivers], and all [their] property forfeited property forfeited, this being the price of his loyalty to the king.[6]

In January 1645, the Parliamentary Committee of both Kingdoms – England and Scotland – created the New Model Army. This was a professional army with many former soldiers among its ranks. Members of all religions or none, were welcome, but no serving Member of Parliament was permitted to enlist.

On the 14 June 1645, King Charles and his army were decisively defeated at the Battle of Naseby, in which the New Model Army was commanded by Sir Thomas Fairfax. Four days later

encouraged by the tidings of that success, Captain Butler, then Governor of Wareham, marched from thence with a party of horse, and, with these driving the garrison into the castle, a company of foot which followed entered the town [of Corfe] bent on pillage, and succeeded in bringing away one hundred and sixty cattle and horses.[7]

In late October 1645, orders were sent

for more effective operations against Corfe Castle. Colonel [John] Bingham, Governor of Poole, had two regiments, [Colonel John] Pickering's and [Colonel Thomas] Rainsborough's, placed at his disposal for this purpose, and on the 16th of December, and again on the 22nd, further reinforcements were sent by [Commander-in-Chief, Sir Thomas] General Fairfax.[8]

For Lady Bankes a ray of hope appeared, in the shape of a young Royalist officer named James Cromwell, a distant relative of the Parliamentary leader, but now his opponent. Hearing of her ladyship's plight, he set off, allegedly from Oxford, with a troop of 125 men and arrived at Wareham, where he captured its governor Captain Butler, together with two members of the Parliamentary Committee. He now proceeded to Corfe, where he offered to escort Lady Bankes to safety. Needless to say, his offer was declined! Cromwell was subsequently captured, together with some of his men. Others took refuge in the castle. Lady Bankes was now to be the victim of betrayal.

The captive Governor of Wareham prevailed on Colonel [formerly Captain] Lawrence, hitherto so trustworthy and still thought to be so, not only to connive at his escape, but to accompany him in his flight. And there was within the walls another traitor, whose conduct was still more base, and his treachery far more fatal in its consequences.

Lieutenant-Colonel [Thomas] Pitman, an officer in the garrison, had served under the Earl of Inchequin in Ireland, and, being weary of the king's service, let the enemy know that if he might have a protection [a document guaranteeing his safety] he would deliver the place to Parliament, which offer was accepted, transmitted to London, and a protection sent down.

Pitman promised Colonel Henry Anketil, the Governor of Corfe Castle, that he would substantially reinforce the garrison. But unbeknown to Anketil, Pitman, was in cahoots with Colonel Bingham 'who commanded the siege'.

A hundred men were drawn out of Weymouth garrison, who marched to Lulworth Castle, where they were joined by thirty or forty more. Pitman led them in the night to the post agreed upon for their entrance, where Colonel Anketil was ready to receive them: some of them were in disguise, and knew every part of the castle. When fifty were entered, the Governor, seeing more behind, ordered the port [gate] to be shut, saying there were as many as he could dispose of. Pitman expostulated with him for using him so ill, by causing him to bring men so far, with the hazard of their lives, and expose them to the cold and the enemy.

The outcome was that the Rebels were granted entry, and the castle was overthrown.

The risk now became imminent of a general slaughter throughout the castle. Colonel Bingham, however, who was no hireling officer, but a descendant of a family long known and highly respected in the county, could not but admire the courage of the lady [Bankes] who was his foe, and he succeeded in preserving the lives of one hundred and forty persons then within the castle.

In return, 30 Parliamentary prisoners were released by the Royalists. Nevertheless, 'two of the garrison were killed, and one of the besiegers, in this final struggle'.

According to theologian and preacher Joshua Sprigg (or Sprigge), this final siege had lasted for forty-eight days 'during which eleven men were slain'.[9]

The day on which this catastrophe occurred is uncertain… it occurred probably in the last week of the month of February [1646].[10]

Sequel

After the Civil War the ring-and-bailey castle, known as 'The Rings', was referred to as 'Cromwell's Battery', indicating that it was from here that the Parliamentarians had bombarded the castle with cannon fire.[11]

In March 1646 an Act was passed in the House of Commons for the 'slighting' of Corfe Castle i.e. its demolition by mining and explosives, Captain Hughes, Governor of Lulworth Castle was appointed to undertake the task. Whereupon, stone and timber from the castle was appropriated by some of the 'gentlemen' of the county who had supported the Parliamentary cause, and also by the enterprising villagers of Corfe. Lead from the castle roofs was sold to a local plumber.

From the dates of many of Corfe's houses, said Editha Langtree, it is believed 'that they were built from the castle's stones, after Cromwell had knocked it about a bit'. Furthermore, in the house of Hibbs, the bakers, 'there is a marble fireplace which came out of the castle'.

On 5 May 1646 the King put himself in the power of the Scottish army [i.e. surrendered, the Scots having invaded England and taken up defensive positions near to the city of Newcastle] and with his sanction the city of Oxford surrendered on the 24 of June.[12]

On 4 June 1646 the Dorsetshire Committee of Sequestration communicated 'to their superiors in London', the following information in regard to Lady Bankes.

Her husband's estate was sequester'd [confiscated] by us during his lyfe tyme for his delinquency [what the Parliamentarians regarded as the late Sir John Bankes's criminality, in respect of his support for the King], but since his decease she hath petitioned us to [i.e. that she might] enjoy the jointure [estate settled on a wife for the period in which she survives her husband] settled on her before the delinquency of her husband. [However] their Lordships in London were at that time too much occupied in the division of the spoil, to find time for an answer to inquiries which related only to the maintenance of those who have been plundered.[13]

King Charles I was put on trial: the charge being that he

hath traitorously and maliciously levied war against the present Parliament, and the people therein represented… [that the] wicked designs, wars, and evil practices of him, the said Charles Stuart, have been, and are carried on for the advancement and upholding of a personal interest of will, power, and pretended prerogative to himself and his family, against the public interest, common right, liberty, justice, and peace of the people of this nation.[14]

He was convicted, condemned to death and executed by beheading on 30 January 1649 on a scaffold erected on the pavement in front of the Banqueting House, Whitehall.

In that year of 1649, Cromwell declared the establishment of a united Commonwealth [republican period of government] of England, Scotland, and Ireland, with himself as Chairman of its Council of State. For Lady Bankes, the coming of Cromwell to power was not an unmixed blessing.

The widowed heroine of the castle was no longer persecuted for her bravery; the attachment which bound Cromwell with warm affection to his daughters gave him a charitable disposition towards all who were of their sex. Large compositions [sums paid in lieu of a larger obligation] being paid for herself and her children, Lady Bankes was now permitted to receive the annual amount [i.e. income] of her jointure, and although claims upon her were from time to time brought forward in the legal tribunals… she was not in any serious degree molested during the remainder of the period of the commonwealth. She lived long enough to see the restoration of the monarchy, but died within a twelve-month from the accomplishment of that desired event.[15]

In 1650, at the Battle of Dunbar, English parliamentary forces commanded by Cromwell defeated a combined Scottish, French, and Albanian army. Cromwell's Commonwealth, however, was not a success. Parliament, in which a substantial number of Royalists remained, obstructed his reforms and in 1653, he dissolved it. He ruled briefly as head of a Puritan Convention following the implementation of a new Constitution, as Lord Protector. He dissolved Parliament again in 1655, with a view to establishing regional rule in England under 10 major generals. Again, the experiment failed. Cromwell died in 1658 and was succeeded as Lord Protector by his son Richard.

In that year, Ralph Bankes was returned by the electorate of Corfe as Member of Richard Cromwell's Parliament.

Largely instrumental in securing the return of the monarchy was General George Monck, 1st Duke of Albermarle, who had fought at Cromwell's side in the Battle of Dunbar. The outcome was, that on 29 May 1660, the late King's son acceded to the throne as King Charles II. In that same year, Ralph Bankes was again returned by the electorate of Corfe: this time for the Parliament of King Charles II.

The fortunes of Ralph Bankes now underwent a dramatic change for the better. The new monarch was mindful of the former's loyalty to his late father, and in that year of 1660 he was knighted. He was also 'permitted to recover the estates forfeited by his delinquent father if he could', just as long as these estates had not been assigned elsewhere, which evidently they had not.[16]

Lady Bankes had spent her final years in London, presumably with her mother and namesake Mary, now a widow, at Ruislip; and also at Damory Court, Blandford Forum, Dorsetshire, home of the Ryves family, which was a mere 9 miles distant from her son Ralph's estate at Kingston Lacy. She died on 11 April 1661 and was buried at Saint Martin's church, Ruislip. The inscription on her tombstone states that she

HAD THE HONOR TO HAVE BORNE WITH
A CONSTANCY AND COURAGE ABOVE HER SEX A
NOBLE PROPORCON OF THE LATE CALAMITIES, AND
THE HAPPINESS TO HAVE OUTLIVED THEM SO FAR
AS TO HAVE SEENE THE RESTITUTION OF THE
GOVERNMENT WITH GREAT PEACE OF MIND....

Lady Bankes displayed great courage, right up until the very end. Even though her death was expected, she had not informed her son Sir Ralph, who was shortly due to be married, that she was unwell. In fact, she died on the very same day that Ralph married Mary Brune of Athelhampton.[17]

In 1663, Ralph set about having a house built for himself at Kingston Lacy near Wimborne - this estate having been purchased by his late father in 1632. Prior to this it had been the seat of the Dukes of Somerset.[18] The house was designed by architect Sir Roger Pratt, and he named it 'Kingston Hall'. (It later became known as Kingston Lacy.) On its walls Ralph hung paintings by fashionable artists such as Sir Anthony van Dyck and Sir Peter Lely, and occupying pride of place in the saloon was a van Dyck portrait of Queen Henrietta Maria, widow of the late King Charles I, which had been presented to his father Sir John, by the late king himself. In other paintings, members of the Bankes family were depicted.

Above the chimney piece in the library, Ralph hung the keys and seals of Corfe Castle, which Colonel Bingham had allowed his mother to retain after the siege. He was also in possession of a horseman's spur and some cannon-balls from the siege.

Some items lost after the castle had fallen to the Rebels and been plundered, were recalled to mind by 'an old servant of the family who had lived in the castle',[19] and he made a list of them. They included

Hangings of watchet damask, green plush, pentado, tapestry, and scarlett & gilt leather; Turkish and Persian carpets; a very large trunke, inlay'd all over with mother of pearle; one [trunk] of crimson plushe, with 2 fair silver and gold laces; many bookes and papers at ye value of 1300l., all new and good...; a large suit of crimson velvet chairs, stooles, couch embroydered, long cushions of crimson velvet; 6 large down & five feather beds with bolsters; some crimson damask curtains, and long cushions for a couch.[20]

This is to name but few of the items, and it indicates the lavish manner in which the castle was furnished in former times. It also surely gives an indication that red and crimson were Lady Bankes's favourite colours! However, few, if any, of these items were ever recovered.

Eight
THE CLAY INDUSTRY

Today the area to the south-west of the Wareham to Corfe road, consists of woodland and heathland which is largely undisturbed, except for occasional lakes which are, in fact, worked out opencast clay mines. However, in the nineteenth century, this area was a hive of activity.

Corfe Castle was an important source of labour for the local clay-mining industry: the nearest clay pits being at Norden, less than a mile away to the north.

The discovery of pre-Roman pottery kilns at Shipstal Point in Purbeck, and at other sites along the southern shoreline of Poole Harbour, indicates that clay was mined locally in the Iron Age period (circa 750 BCE to 43 CE). In Purbeck the Durotriges (a people who inhabited Dorset during the Iron Age) made Black Burnished Ware – black or grey and with a coarse, gritty texture. The Romans also produced such ware following their invasion of 43, and such production continued until the Roman withdrawal of 410 and beyond.

Purbeck clay is known as 'ball clay' (allegedly because the traditional, narrow spades which were used to dig it out were called 'tubals'). Sedimentary in origin, it was formed some 45 million years, or so, ago during the Eocene epoch, when kaolinite from eroded granite from Dartmoor in Devonshire, was carried to Purbeck in an ancient river system. It is to be found to the north of the ridge of Purbeck hills in lens-shaped deposits 15 – 20 feet thick and up to several acres in area, at depths of up to 200 feet.

The Romans dug clay from an area immediately to the east of Norden, and many of their kilns have been discovered: an indication that pottery was produced here on an industrial scale.

Purbeck ball clay is highly sought after, even to this day, because the small and uniform size of its grains means that when mixed with china clay (a fine, white clay used in the making of ceramics) it gives the finished chinaware product an added plasticity and strength. It also has the advantage of turning white when fired.

There were two principal reasons why the Purbeck clay-mining industry flourished. The first was the introduction of tobacco into England in the mid-1560s and its subsequent popularization by English courtier Sir Walter Raleigh: hence a sudden and universal demand for clay pipes. The second was the introduction, in 1657, of tea to Britain from China: hence the demand for 'china' crockery, which fast began to replace existing wood or pewter vessels and plates in the home. In consequence the pottery towns of the

English Midlands (known as 'The Potteries') in particular, underwent rapid expansion. Ball clay was also traditionally used in sugar refining.

From the sixteenth century various families, notably those of Brown, Hyde, and Garland, rented land from Purbeck landowners in order to mine clay. The procedure was as follows. First, the vegetation and topsoil were removed and the clay dug out with long, narrow spades – 'tubals'. As the mine grew deeper, stepped sides were created for ease of working.

At first, clay was dug from opencast pits, but when the surface deposits became exhausted, operations moved to below ground: 'below ground' workers being paid more than those who worked 'above ground'.

Joseph Pike (born 1723) of Ranscombe Estate, Chudleigh was a merchant and ship owner involved in the ball-clay industry (Devonshire's Bovey Basin bordering the River Teign, being the other principal source of ball clay in Britain). In 1756 he married Katherine Westcott of Chudleigh. In the late eighteenth century he commenced ball-clay mining operations in the vicinity of Furzebrook, 2 miles to the north-west of Corfe and in the parish of Church Knowle. From here clay was laboriously transported 2½ miles across the heath from Furzebrook to Ridge, situated half a mile downstream from Wareham on the River Frome; first by donkeys fitted with panniers, and later by horse-drawn waggons. Here, it was left to 'weather'.

The weathering process involved large mounds of clay being dumped in weathering beds, left exposed to the elements for several months, and turned from time to time. This improved its plasticity and cleansed it of impurities. (This process was subsequently superseded by machine shredding.) Finally, the clay was transported by rowing boat (and in latter years by sailing-barge) down the tortuous River Frome and Wareham Channel to Poole. Here, it was transferred to larger, sea-going ships for the voyage to Liverpool and then on to the Staffordshire potteries, by way of the Grand Trunk Canal; or to potteries in London, Glasgow, and elsewhere, and abroad to the Continent. Soon, an ever-increasing number of opencast pits were being opened in Purbeck over an area of several square miles.

Joseph Pike's sons John William Pike (born 1759) and William Joseph Pike (born 1761), also relocated from their home town of Chudleigh to Purbeck: the former to Wareham and the latter to Corfe Castle. In 1790, William Joseph Pike was living at Market Street, Corfe in company with a writing clerk, a woman servant, and three clay cutters.[1] John and William subsequently founded the firm, Pike Brothers of Wareham.

In 1791 articles of agreement were signed, whereby William Joseph Pike undertook to supply 1200 tons of Purbeck ball clay annually for five years to Josiah Wedgwood, Potter of Etruria near Stoke-on-Trent, and to other Staffordshire potters for the sum of £120. Articles of Agreement of a similar

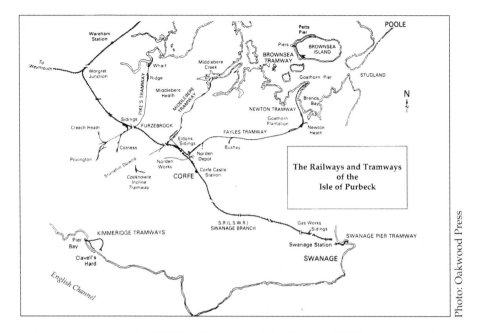

nature were signed in 1798 by Wedgwood & Co with William, his brother John, and their father, Joseph Pike.

By now, Wedgwood had achieved international recognition by supplying Empress Catherine the Great of Russia, in 1774, with a 952 piece dinner service of 'Queen's Ware' – cream coloured earthenware.

In 1798, William Joseph Pike acquired from Lewis Cockram Esquire of Swanage, the lease of Bucknowle House, situated on the edge of Corfe Common near Church Knowle.[2] The Pikes' connection to the Potteries was not simply a commercial one, for in 1803, William married Ann Warburton of Cobridge, Staffordshire. She bore him seven children.

The Pikes had a rival in Benjamin Fayle, a Dublin merchant and insurance broker, born in 1751, who had relocated to London and lived with his wife Charlotte and family at Dulwich.[3] His company, Benjamin Fayle & Co. Ltd., had been in existence since 1795.

In 1803, Fayles took control of clay pits at Norden, a mile or so to the north of Corfe, from which village the company largely drew its workforce. The pits had been formerly worked by Thomas Hyde. From here, clay was transported by packhorse across 2½ miles of heath to Middlebere Creek, on the shores of Poole Harbour.

In 1806, Fayle revolutionized the method of transporting clay by linking Norden to Middlebere by a 2½-mile-long 'plateway' – which differed from a railway in that it was the rails, and not the waggons' wheels which were flanged. The rails were of cast iron, 3 feet in length and L-shaped; the vertical flange being on the outside. The gauge was 3ft 9in.

The end of each rail had two bosses on its underside which fitted into two indentations in the stone block on which it rested. Into this block a hole had been drilled, and into this hole was inserted an oak plug with hollowed out core. Into this plug a metal spike was driven, which held the ends of the two rails together. (There were no 'sleepers', as such, linking the two lines of track.)[4]

The balls of clay were loaded into waggons and transported to the perimeter of the pit, there to be reloaded into the larger waggons of the plateway, where a team of two horses hauled five waggons – each carrying two tons of clay.[5] At Middlebere the clay was left for a month to weather, prior to being shipped by barge down the Wytch Channel to Poole Harbour. Three return journeys were made daily, enabling approximately 10,000 tons of ball clay to be exported annually. From now on, not only the clay mines, but also the Middlebere Plateway, provided employment for the people of Corfe and district.

In 1807 new deposits of clay were discovered at Norden, to the west of the Corfe-to-Wareham road. Two tunnels were therefore built, in order to link them to the plateway. Passing places were also created on the line: innovations which enabled the annual output of clay to be doubled.

In 1812 the clay waggons were fitted with Collinge axles (invented by John Collinge of Lambeth in 1792). The wheels now revolved on fixed axles which obviated the need for them to be removed and the axle arms re-greased every day. In about 1815, 'Pike Brothers' commenced mining in the Creech area to the west of Corfe.

Benjamin Fayle died in February 1831. Whereupon, his son the Reverend Richard Fayle, his son-in-law Benjamin G. Babington (husband of Anna Maria Fayle), and his daughter Charlotte, carried on the business.

Joseph Pike died at Chudleigh in 1810. Ann Pike died in 1831 and her husband William Joseph Pike, died in 1833 which was evidently when the Pike connection with Bucknowle House ceased. John William Pike of Wareham, died in 1840. Both Pike brothers, William and John, are buried at Church Knowle.

In that year of 1840, Pikes constructed a tramway of their own. Allegedly of 4ft gauge, it ran in a straight line from Furzebrook to Ridge and had the advantage of being largely gravity assisted. Thus, virtually all the horses were required to do was to haul the empty waggons back up the slope after delivery. As the Pikes expanded their operations westwards, this line was linked to clay pits at Creech, Cotness, Greenspecks and Povington.

A new generation of Pikes now took charge of the business: namely, William

Joseph and Ann Pike's sons William Joseph Pike (junior) and John William Pike (who presumably were twins, both having been born at Bucknowle in 1813).[6] In 1841, according to census records, the population of Corfe included 23 clay cutters and a clerk of clay works, out of a total population of about 1000.

In 1843, William Joseph Pike (junior) married Anna Lewis (born Dorchester 1824, the daughter of clergyman Lewis Lewis) and the couple lived at North Street, Wareham. In 1848[7] William Joseph's brother John William Pike, married Mary Mayer (born 1839, daughter of Staffordshire potter Thomas Mayer and his wife Charlotte), and the couple lived first at Oak Cottage, Parkstone and subsequently at Westport, Wareham.

Since the early 1850s, Fayles had been mining clay at Goathorn (3½ miles to the north-east of Corfe and 2½ miles to the east of Middlebere) in the parish of Studland, and near to the southern shores of Poole Harbour. In 1852 a pier was built at the end of the Goathorn peninsula, a mile or so to the north, and in April 1854 this was linked to Newton (a hamlet situated in the heart of the Goathorn clayworks) by tramway, gauge 3ft 9in.[8] The Norden-to-Goathorn line became known as Fayle's Tramway.

In 1866, Pike's converted their Ridge tramway to a railway, gauge 2ft 8in, and replaced the horses by steam-powered locomotives. This was probably through the influence of railway engineer George Stephenson, with whom William Pike (junior) was acquainted. The first of these locomotives was *Primus*, to be followed later by *Secundus*, *Tertius* and so forth over the years; ending with *Septimus*. By now, a steam-driven tug hauled five barges laden with clay down the River Frome to Poole.

Meanwhile, as the clay-mining community at Goathorn grew, clay miners' cottages and a school were built. In 1868, Fayle's Tramway was regauged to 3ft 9in and the steam locomotive *Tiny*, introduced to work the line.

In 1874, William Pike (junior) purchased the 1000-acre Furzebrook Estate from the trustees of the Brown family. (It is not known when clay mining commenced on this land, but in 1578 the heathland which subsequently became the Furzebrook Estate, had been purchased by John Brown and John Barter from Christopher Perry. By the 1660s, Brown's grandson Thomas, was 'actively engaged in selling clay for making tobacco pipes'.[9])

The estate included a farm and farmhouse, together with 'pits and mines of tobacco pipe, potters', and sugar bakers' clay'.[10] William Pike duly had the farmhouse demolished and built a mansion, Furzebrook House, on the site.

In about 1881 new pits were opened up at Norden. When a rail link from Wareham to Swanage was proposed, Fayle's Middlebere Plateway was extended so as to run adjacent and parallel to it. And when the branch line was duly opened by the London & South Western Railway (LSWR) in 1885, the creation of 'Lord Eldon's Clayworks Sidings' made it possible for clay to be transferred to the main line. (Lord Eldon – John Scott, 1845-1926, 3rd Earl of Eldon, landowner of Encombe in South Dorsetshire.) At about this time, Fayles opened up new clay workings at Arfleet, ½ mile to the north-west of Corfe, which were now linked to Fayle's Tramway.[11]

By 1890, Pikes had expanded their mining operations further westwards from Furzebrook, as far as Cotness and West Creech.

In 1901, 32 clay-industry workers were residents of Corfe, including three clay cutters (above ground); 12 clay miners (underground); a foreman of clay works; a wood sawyer of clay works; 14 clay-pit labourers (above ground); and a borer of clay pits (above ground).[12]

In respect of underground working

> *Two methods are in use, depending on the depth and alignment of the clay deposits. The waggons either come up a vertical shaft in a hoist fitted with rails, or they are cable-hauled up a steep incline. These inclines are sometimes of considerable length, a typical one… being about 250 yards long, with an average gradient of just under 1 in 6. At the surface, waggons are run into a high-level transhipment shed and the clay is tipped down chutes into the waiting transport below.[13]*

In about 1907, Fayles built a 3-mile tramway of 3ft 9in gauge to link Norden to Newton, and hence to connect with Fayle's Tramway. *Tiny*, which 'could not take the gradients across the heath, was replaced by the larger steam locomotive *Thames*, and relegated to shunting duties at Eldon Sidings'.[14] The Middlebere Plateway was now dispensed with.

Corfe Castle from the nearby Arfleet clay works. Photo: Bob Richards

During the First World War, clay mining was a 'reserved occupation'. The miners were therefore not called up to join the armed forces – clay being needed to make moulds for shells and bombs. In the 1920s clay extraction at Goathorn began to decline.[15] Today, there is virtually no indication that a community of over 50 people once lived and worked here.

Ada Cooper recalled how, when the little (clay) train arrived at the main Corfe to Wareham road, it would be preceded by a man with a red flag who held up the road traffic in order for the train to cross. This was a reference to the railway line which linked clay workings on the west side of the road, south of Norden Farm, to Fayle's Tramway on the east side.

In the 1930s, instead of the long, tubal, hand-held spades, pneumatic spades were introduced and the waggons which brought the clay to the surface were hauled by electrically-driven winches.

The last owner of Furzebrook House and Estate was Leonard Gaskell Pike.[16] In 1935, Thomas T. Barnard (formerly Director of the School of African Life and Languages at Cape Town University) and his wife Lilian Barnard, acquired the property. Within the estate was a large lake (one of the Pikes' former opencast mines which had become flooded) and Barnard hit on the idea of turning it, together with its 25 acres of surrounding heathland, into a tourist attraction. The 'Blue Pool' was opened in that same year. It is now a Site of Special Scientific Interest, with museum, gift shop and café. In 1939, the Norden-to-Goathorn line was closed, but the lines around Norden remained in use (until 1971).

During the Second World War much of the heath was taken over by the army and used as a firing range, leading to the closure, in 1940, of the Pikes' Ridge railway. In 1948 the Norden lines were converted to 2ft gauge, and *Thames* was replaced by *Russell*. 'Steel tipper' waggons were now used.[17] In 1949 the two companies Pike and Fayle, merged under the name of 'Pike Brothers, Fayle & Co.'

In 1954 the Pike railway's tracks were re-gauged to 2ft and worked by diesel locomotives. Shortly afterwards the decision was taken to transport clay by road, rather than by rail.

In 1968 the company was acquired by English China Clays (ECC).

In 1999 ECC was acquired by the French company, Imerys. In the same year mining operations at Norden ceased. Imerys operated five opencast clay pits in Purbeck and a central storage and processing works at Furzebrook: ball clay being exported mainly to Spain, Italy, and elsewhere on the Continent. Because it can withstand high temperatures and has high tensile strength, the clay is also used, for example, for high-voltage insulators; for plastic coatings on flexible cables; and for kiln furniture (used to support and separate objects which are being fired).

Nine
THE INFLUENCE OF
WILLIAM MORTON PITT

W illiam Morton Pitt (1754-1836) of Kingston House near Dorchester, was an MP and a philanthropist. In 1789 he announced that he proposed to conduct a census of Corfe and district. It was Pitt's opinion that such a census would provide 'great parochial advantages', and 'great national benefit would result therefrom'.

> *This would enable the Clergyman, Parish Officers, Vestry, and Contributors to the Poor's Rates in general, in any place, to form a perfect judgment on the situation and wants of every distressed person or family, to discriminate between the deserving, and dissolute or idle, and to provide employment for those who are in want of it, and especially for children, as they become successively able to undertake any work.[1]*

In 1790, Pitt's census of Corfe was duly published. It is useful because it allows a comparison to be made between the occupations of the villagers in that year, and in the year of the 1901 National Census – over a century later.

In 1790 the population of Corfe was just over 700, and the percentage of the population that was engaged in the following occupations was as follows: spinners (who spun wool into yarn for weaving) and knitters (who knitted stockings etc.) and who were exclusively women and girls, 12%; clay-industry employees, 8%; building industry 4%; domestic servants, 3%; shoemakers and labourers, each 2%; carpenters and blacksmiths, each 1.5%; tailors 1%; publicans, 0.7%. In that year 5% of the population was on 'parish pay' (relief, paid by the parish to those in need). Only two persons were of 'independent means'.

Other occupations included tallow chandler (vendor of rendered animal fat, suitable for making candles); house painter; barber; lime burner; thatcher; fellmonger (dealer in hides or skins); hurdler; furze cutter; glazier; mantua (gown) maker; and fisherman (surprisingly for an inland village). No one in the village was classified as a farmer.

The rector was the Reverend Sir Thomas Bankes l'Anson, sixty-six, widower, and a direct descendant of Lady Bankes of Civil War fame. The curate was the Reverend John Gent, forty-nine, married. The postman was Robert Beere, sixty-seven, married.

8.5% of the population were working children under the age of sixteen

William Morton Pitt,
engraving after C. W. Day.
Courtesy National Trust

years – 60 in all. For example, Joseph Keats, eleven, quarrier; William Hustens, eleven, saddler; John Luther, twelve, carpenter; John Hibbs, thirteen, clay cutter; Rebecca Gould, ten, knits; William Langtree, thirteen, breeches maker; George White, eight, labourer; Ann Ralls, thirteen, spins worsted (smooth yarn, spun from wool).

Pitt's 1790 census also contains the following interesting information. Hannah Trent, twenty-eight, 'husband run away, she on parish pay'; Ruth Maclean, forty-two 'husband absconded, knits, she is on parish pay'; Mary Hibbs, sixteen 'bastard daughter of Ursula Welsh, an idiot, spins, on parish pay'; Richard Davy, thirty-one 'cuts furze, foolish'; Matthew Hayward, forty, 'clay cutter, almost an idiot'. Thomas Bushrod, thirty-six, widower, mason is recorded as 'dying of consumption'. Publican Joseph Luther, was also a carpenter, and publican John Conway was also a barber.

In 1901 the population of Corfe was just over 820, and the percentage of the population that was engaged in the following occupations was as follows: clay industry, 4% (compared with 8% in 1790); building industry and dressmaking, 2% each; domestic servants, 1.5%; carpenters, grocers, general labourers, gardeners, and railway employees, 1% each; teachers, postal workers, and blacksmiths, 0.7% each; doctors and nurses 0.5%; publicans, 0.4%. Ten persons were of independent means. There is no record of any person being in receipt of parish pay. And there is no record of any child under the age of fourteen being in employment, the reason being that they were now attending school (see below).

Other occupations listed in 1901 included: reading-room caretaker; professor of music; agent to the Prudential Assurance Company; relieving officer (appointed to administer relief to the poor)/vaccination officer (against smallpox)/school attendance officer (combined); paraffin oil merchant; clergymen (of whom there were three); a sergeant of police; post office clerk; stationery engine driver (who presumably worked at the clay mine). Only two farmers appear in the census: James Willshire of East Street and Reginald Crofts (poultry farmer) of Market Place (now known as 'The Square'). Only seven agricultural labourers were listed.

Except for members of the professions, retirement, either in 1790 or in 1901, does not appear to have been an option, unless on the grounds of ill health or infirmity,[2] For example, William White, seventy-three, widower, is listed in 1790 as 'mole catcher'. What conclusions may be drawn by comparing these two censuses of 1790 and 1901?

i. Education
The fact that there is no record of any child being in employment in 1901, reflects the fact that the Education Acts of 1880, 1891, 1893, and 1899, made school attendance for children compulsory.

ii. Poverty
Corfe's present almshouses (almshouse – a house founded by charity, offering accommodation for the poor[3]), situated in East Street and originally for six 'aged persons', dates from not earlier than the eighteenth century. However, 'a hospital called the almshouse' is mentioned in a document of 1566.[4]

The 'Poor Law' refers to a system for the relief of England's poor, established by the Poor Relief Act of 1601. By the Act, each parish became responsible for its poor, who were maintained by parish taxes. The Poor Law was supervised by Justices of the Peace and administered by overseers.

The will of Sir Edmund Uvedale, MP (a cousin of the aforementioned John Uvedale), who died in 1606, stated that the sum of £5 was to be given to the churchwardens of Corfe

> *to be employed as a stock to set the poor on work according to the statute for the relief of the poor.*

Corfe's Almshouses. Photo: Bob Richards

70

In other words, the poor were encouraged to earn their keep. To the same churchwardens and their successors, Sir Edmund

> *devised [bequeathed] all lands of Sharpford, New Mills, and Derby lands within the parish of Corfe Castle, unto Sir John Ryves, knt [knight], Sir Nathaniel Napper, knt, and Richard Swayne, esq. and their heirs, towards the maintenances of the poor of the almshouse of the borough of Corfe Castle for ever.*[5]

By 1796, Uvedale House (1575, formerly Place House, and later an inn, the King's Arms, situated in lower East Street – otherwise known as Bridge Street) had come into the possession of the Bankes family, when it was agreed that the property should be used to house the poor of the village. It now became known as 'Poor House Yard'.

In 1834, the Poor Law Amendment Act decreed as follows. If a person who was neither on the 'medical pauper list' of the parish, nor in the workhouse (both of which had their own arrangements), became sick or injured, the medical officer appointed to attend the parish

> *shall promptly afford to the said sick or injured person the necessary medical relief, and shall continue to do so until that person shall have recovered.*

If, after three months, recovery had not occurred, 'a new order shall be obtained'.[6]

Workhouses were public institutions in which the destitute of a parish received board and lodging in return for work. A workhouse would normally have its own 'sick ward'. For greater economy and efficiency, parishes were grouped into 'Unions'. The Poor Law Union for Purbeck (or 'Purbeck Union') was formed on 25 March 1836, and that September it merged with Wareham to form the Wareham and Purbeck Union. In the following year, 1837, the Union Workhouse was built at Wareham, this being the nearest purpose-built workhouse to Corfe.

In 1843, Corfe's almshouses contained an unspecified number of 'paupers' – very poor people who were recipients of poor relief.[7] In the following years Corfe's almshouses were stated to be the property of the churchwardens of Corfe,[8] which perhaps had always been the case.

iii. Health
What help could the people of Corfe expect from the medical profession in the year 1790, if they could not afford to pay for private treatment? The answer is that the local doctor would be paid by the parish to attend them.

Ten
EDUCATION

The children of the wealthy were traditionally educated by a governess: the boys being sent to preparatory school, and subsequently to 'public' i.e. private – school, when they attained the age of twelve or thirteen years.

In 1790 there was one schoolmaster in Corfe – Richard Taylor, thorty-seven, married, of Market Place – whose school had seven boarders. And there were two schoolmistresses; Miriam House, forty-five, widow, of Market Place whose school had one boarder, and Ann Jones, sixty, widow, of Back [West] Street. The location of these schools is not known. The fact that they had boarders indicates that they were fee paying.

Almost three decades later, in 1818, the Select Committee on Education for the Poor recorded the existence of two schools at Corfe, one a day school, and the other for boarders, each with about 30 pupils.[1]

For the majority of children, the education system in England was framed by various Education Acts of Parliament, passed between 1880 and 1899. The Elementary Education Act of 1880 made school attendance compulsory for children aged between five and ten years. Nonetheless, poor families, being dependent on the extra wage that their children brought in, tended to send them out to work regardless. For this reason, attendance officers were appointed to check up on such children. With compulsory schooling, said Editha Langtree, the Dame Schools (small, primary schools, usually run by elderly women) were done away with.

Children between the ages of ten and thirteen who were employed, were required to produce a certificate to show they had reached a certain educational standard.

The 1891 Elementary Education Act provided for payment of school fees by the state of ten shillings per head per annum. The Elementary Education (School Attendance) Act of 1893, raised the minimum school leaving age to eleven, and in 1899 the age was raised, once again, to thirteen.

Most state-educated children were taught either in National Schools, or in British Schools (see below). National Schools were founded by the National Society for Promoting the Education of the Poor in the Principles of the Established Church of England and Wales, which was created in the year 1811.

Corfe's Church of England National School was built on the west side of East Street in 1834. The school's first headmaster was Lackford Hart Langtree (1806-1870), Editha's uncle, who subsequently also became a collector of the Poor Rates (taxes raised to provide relief for the poor) in the parish. Langtree married Maria Hooper in 1832 in Wareham, and the couple had 10 children, all born in Corfe.

In 1895 the Bankes Memorial School was built on the opposite side of the road to the National School, to cater for the senior pupils. Meanwhile, the latter school continued to be used for the infants, from five to eight years of age, with Miss Card as headmistress. Elizabeth Roe Card, the daughter of Edward Card (schoolmaster of Cerne Abbas in West Dorsetshire) and his wife Susan Ann Roe, was born at Corfe in 1860. Assisted by a junior teacher, she would occupy this post for forty-six years.

The Bankes Memorial School, whose headmaster from 1915 was Mr Rupert G. Matthews, took children from nine to fourteen years of age. Pupils, who numbered about 100, came not only from Corfe, but also from surrounding villages.

Ada Cooper, a former pupil of the Bankes Memorial School, described how the pupils were summoned from the playground by the ringing of the school bell, whereupon the boys and girls would line up and march indoors for 'Assembly', which was held in the main hall. After prayers and the singing of a hymn, they would then disperse to their separate classrooms. However, pupils who belonged to the Methodist Church were excused assembly.

The older children, said Ada

used pen and ink for their school work, and the younger ones had slate pencils and slates. The job of filling the ink wells was a lovely, messy job, done by one of the older children.

For the girls, lessons included needlework and cookery, and for the boys, there were painting lessons.

In our singing lessons, we learned all the old, traditional songs:
God Bless the Prince of Wales; Men of Harlech; The Oak and the Ash, *and* Rule Britannia.

Favourite playground games for the girls were hopscotch, rounders, and handball. Meanwhile, the boys played football, either here, or at the West Street football pitch.

Ada recalled being taken on nature walks to Corfe Common, where she and her fellow pupils 'would find and identify flowers and plants such as viper's bugloss, sundew, and various orchids.

'Bright children,' said Ada, sat an examination at the age of ten, which if they passed, gained them entrance to Poole, Parkstone, or Dorchester Grammar School, sometimes on a scholarship. However, when Swanage

Grammar School was opened in 1929, this was far more convenient. As for the remainder, they left school at the age of fourteen and started work.

On Empire Day 24 May each year, 'the pupils paraded with flags and sang patriotic songs'.[2]

A box of books was delivered to the school every Friday from the County Library. This 'was the only source of reading matter for the general public'. The travelling library did not come to the village until the 1950s or 1960s. Finally, in the 1970s, a new library was built.

Infants continued to be taught at the National School until the late 1950s, whereupon, the ground floor became the Bankes Memorial School's canteen. As for the first floor, this was purchased by the Reverend Batley for use as a church hall.[3] Here, social functions, including dances were held. In 1977 the building was acquired by the Royal British Legion.

Some time prior to 1880, Fayles had created a private school at Goathorn for the education of the children of the company's clayworkers. By 1903 the school complex consisted of schoolhouse and schoolteacher's cottage. There were 25 pupils; the schoolmistress was Ellen Joyce, and the school was now open to all.

By 1930, with the decline of the Newton clayworks, Goathorn School had closed and pupils, whose numbers had by now declined, were obliged to walk to school at Studland. This was in all weathers and in the winter months, it meant journeying to-and-fro in the dark.

In September 1933, following protests by parents, Fayles, in agreement with Dorset County Council, agreed to lay on a 'passenger train' in order to convey the children from Goathorn to Arfleet.

> Ten children from Goathorn have hitherto had to walk 3 miles to school, but the china clay firm which employs their fathers is now providing transport daily [to Corfe] in each direction by rail.

The make up of the train was as follows. The locomotive employed was *Thames*, and

> the 'passenger coach' [number '78'] appears to be one of the china clay waggons on which there has been erected a primitive wooden structure with a corrugated iron roof and a window in the neighbourhood of the roof which provides more light than it does enjoyment of the view. The interior of the 'carriage' is fitted up with a wooden seat. The train reaches Corfe at 8.50 in the morning, and returns at 4 in the afternoon, taking about 20 minuites in each direction.

The Newton to Arfleet 'School Train', 3 May 1934, photographed by S. P. W. Corbett. Sisters June Surface (on left) and Joyce Surface (on right), standing beside the track. Already aboard (left to right) Elsie Surface, boy pupil Fennel, Pamela Foot, and Eileen Surface.

The passenger waggon was nicknamed the 'Hen House', and the cost to the education authority was stated to be 7 shillings and sixpence per day.[4] The sight of the little locomotive puffing its way across the landscape of purple heather, hauling its carriage full of excitable, but invisible young charges, must have been one to behold! The school train having deposited the pupils at Arfleet, they alighted, and

> crossed the trestle bridge over the Corfe River and walked the mile to school in Corfe village.[5]

The school train was captured on film by photographer Simon P. W. Corbett.

Bushey, in the parish of Corfe Castle, lies 1½ miles to the east of the village. Its clay workings were linked to Fayle's Tramway by a branch line. Bushey School was built in 1836. When it closed in 1927 its pupils caught the aforementioned school train, which passed within a stone's throw of the hamlet.

On rainy days the pupils would arrive at their school in East Street, soaking wet, and be obliged to hang their coats out to dry on the guard rails which surrounded the coal or coke-burning 'Tortoise' stoves, of which there was one in each classroom.

From April 1937 the children of Goathorn attended school at Studland, to which they were conveyed by taxi.[6] When the area was taken over by the

Infant's School, Corfe, circa 1900. Photo Barbara Cannings

military at the beginning of the Second World War, Goathorn School was virtually destroyed. In 1956, it was rebuilt as Goathorn Farmhouse.[7] As for Bushey School, it survives to this day as a private residence.

Corfe's British [Nonconformist] School

British Schools were founded by the British and Foreign School Society, created in 1808. They were non-denominational (i.e. not restricted as regards religious denomination); dedicated to the education of the poor, and supported by evangelical and non-conformist (not conforming to the doctrine of the established, Anglican Church) Christians.

It was George Hubbard, Minister of Corfe's Congregational chapel from 1827, who, together with his friends, arranged that the chapel at Well Court, West Street, be used as a 'British (Nonconformist) School' during weekdays.[8]

Even after the new Congregational chapel was built in East Street in 1835, 'the British School was continued in the old leasehold chapel [at Well Court] for many years'.[9] In 1840 headmaster of the British School was James Tucker, who was also the postmaster.[10] The British School closed in the early 1870s.

Eleven
HEALTH PROVISION

A comparison of censuses demonstrates that in 1790, Corfe's only medical personnel were John Keynton, aged sixty-three, married, surgeon, and Ann Dowdale, thirty-five, married, 'practices surgery'. Incidentally, the 1790 census states that Thomas Bushrod, aged thirty-six, mason and widower, was dying at home of consumption (tuberculosis). It was not until 1855 that the purpose-built Royal National Sanatorium was built in Bournemouth with 97 beds for 'consumptive patients'.

In 1841, the Dorset County Hospital – a charitable institution for the treatment of the working poor – was established.

The first of Corfe's doctors who Editha Langtree remembered was Dr William E. Humble, 'and I had cause to', she said. The year was 1877, when she was aged five and her brother Alfred ('Alf') was aged seven. They were playing with the chaff cutter – a mechanical device for chopping hay and straw for use as fodder – said Editha, when Alf reached under the knife

to take out something. I turned the handle, which cut off one finger. Dr Humble ran after me down the yard and threatened me with his stick.

She hid behind the door. 'I was very frightened'.

By 1901, according to the census, Corfe's medical personnel had increased considerably and included Toft Barker, twenty-eight, married, surgeon and physician; May J. Orchard, fifty-five, widow, 'midwife and monthly nurse'; Elisabeth Talbot, sixty-three, widow, 'monthly nurse'; Geraldine J. Fardell, twenty-two, single, 'nurse lady'; Harriet Gover, forty-five, single, 'occasional nurse'.

Dr Toft Barker was the first person in the village to own a motorcycle, said Editha. That was in the first decade of the twentieth century.

He fell off it by the Drug Stores. The doctor was ruined by a man named Candy at Encombe. He taught him to drink, and that finished him.

But not quite, for the doctor subsequently relocated to London.[1]

Ada Cooper described how, as a child in the early twentieth century, she was given a spoonful of Golden Syrup each morning, or plain boiled rice mixed with flowers of sulphur (a powdered form of sulphur formed by sublimation) 'to cleanse the blood'. In winter, she was given camphorated oil, which was considered to be 'the remedy for sore throats and coughs. This

was always in a blue or dark-green bottle, 'to show it must be rubbed on the chest, not drunk'.

Dr Godfrey Dru Drury was Dr Toft Barker's successor as Corfe's General Practitioner. Born at Blackheath, Kent in 1880, he was the son of Edward (architect and surveyor) and his wife, Clara (née Drew). Having qualified at St Bartholomew's Hospital, London, Dr Dru Drury came to Corfe in 1906. In that same year, he married a nurse at St Barthomomew's viz. Ethel Blanche Sims of Henley in Warwickshire, who bore him two sons and a daughter. The couple lived in the house in The Square (subsequently known as Drurys), where surgery was held in a wooden hut in the garden.

Dr Godfrey Dru Drury.
Photo: Stephen Dru Drury

In order to sterilize his needles, Dr Dru Drury would take them across the yard to the kitchen and immerse them in boiling water.[2]

Dr Dru Drury also served as Medical Officer and Public Vaccinator for the Wareham and Purbeck Union, and as Honorary Medical Officer to Swanage Cottage Hospital. In his early years he did his rounds on horseback, but latterly, he was one of the first people in the village to own a car – a De Dion Bouton – which he used when visiting patients in outlying districts.

The doctor had a wide range of interests outside medicine. Inspired by his great grandfather Dru Drury (1724-1803), the celebrated entomologist, he too studied insects and butterflies, and amassed a fine collection (now to be seen in the Dorset County Museum). He was the local officer for the Society of Antiquaries and a leading member of the Dorset Natural History and Archaeological Society, for whom he published pamphlets on various subjects, such as local churches (including Corfe's Church of St Edward); early ecclesiastical effigies; Purbeck marble, and thirteenth-century steelyard weights (steelyard – apparatus for weighing). He was also an enthusiastic member of Corfe's cricket team, and its captain from 1906 – 1930.

In the early days, said Editha Langtree, Dr Dru Drury was in practice with two doctors in Swanage, but latterly, he was single-handed. It was,

Corfe's Cricket Team, circa 1910, Captain, Dr Dru Drury (2nd row, 3rd from left).
Photo: Jim Fooks

therefore, hardly surprising that 'he rarely took a holiday'. The doctor had bushy black eyebrows and thick white hair, said Ada Cooper, and his stethoscope was always 'very cold indeed'. However, when he took your temperature and thumped your chest, 'you knew you were going to get better'. The wooden shed in the back garden, which served as the surgery, said Editha

> *was divided into three by wooden partitions: the inner room being the office, where records were kept and examinations were made; the middle section was the dispensary, and the section next to the door was the small waiting room. There was only room for six or eight people at most, sitting facing each other knee-to-knee, and unless the weather was very cold, people preferred to wait their turn outside, where it could be very draughty at times.*
>
> *It was fascinating to watch the doctor make up the medicines – there were not many pills in those days. He had a small pair of scales, and on a piece of paper would weigh out the different crystals or powders, put them into a medicine bottle, add in water from a jug (no water laid on), put the cork in, shake the bottle, wipe, and label. If you were a private patient, the bottle was then wrapped in white paper, but if you were 'on the panel' you got it unwrapped. Medicines that had to be called for were left just inside the back door of the house, and you just opened the door and helped yourself.*

The National Insurance Act of 1911 entitled poor workers to healthcare, contributions being made both by them and by their employers. However, the benefits did not apply to their wives and children; so those who could afford it paid a regular amount weekly to a 'Friendly [Mutual Insurance] Society', in order to provide cover for themselves too. Jim Fooks recalled how the insurance man came round each week to collect his mother's payment of one penny. The 'panel' referred to above was a list of medical practitioners registered in a district as accepting patients under the National Insurance Act.

Mary Wills of Corfe recalled how, whilst waiting in the 'waiting room', 'you could hear everything that was going on in the surgery'! Also, that the good doctor filled up a large enamel jug with water obtained from an outside tap at the rear of the kitchen, and used it to dilute his medicines. Indigestion mixture was white in colour; cough medicine was pink.

Dr Dru Drury was interested in art and painted the coats of arms of the former Constables of Corfe Castle.

Ethel Dru Drury died on 23 November 1933 of typhoid fever. The doctor himself died on 12 October 1966, having been the village's general practitioner for a period of fifty years.

Editha described how, one day, she was out walking across 'The Halves' when she passed through a gate into a field and encountered a horse which evidently believed that she had something in her basket for him to eat. Suddenly, she said

I found myself lying in the ditch, being kicked at the back of the knee. It was so quickly done, I didn't realize the trouble until the pain started.

A policeman was summoned and he advised her to go to the doctor. Country living was not without its dangers!

The 'Halves' (otherwise known as 'The Hawes') is an area of open land between East Street and West Street. For a fee, payable to the landowner (the principal ones being Bankes, Bond, and Calcraft), the villager could rent a plot of land on The Halves on which to graze his or her 'milk cow' or donkey. Each plot was marked by a stone bearing the leaseholder's initials.

On 5 July 1948 the National Health Service – a publicly funded healthcare system for the United Kingdom – was founded.

Corfe's almshouses survive to the present day. They were modernized in 1977 and named Jubilee House; that being the year of Queen Elizabeth II's Silver Jubilee. Ada Cooper stated that the conditions in the almshouses in East Street were very primitive prior to their modernization. She remembered one resident in particular,

Old Mr Tomes, who had a club foot, and who got so dirty he shone, as if he had been polished with black boot polish.[3]

Twelve
THE RAILWAY

In May 1840, the London and South Western Railway (LSWR) linked London, the capital to the city of Southampton. In 1847, the LSWR opened the newly-created line linking Southampton with Dorchester.

John Mowlem was born on 12 October 1788 at Carrants Court (Court Hill), Swanage. He grew up to be a Quarryman, following in the footsteps of his father John (senior).

The men and boys who worked the multitude of small, family-owned, underground quarries, dug at an angle of 45 degrees and a depth of 50 feet, or so, into the Swanage hillside. They hewed out the stone by the light of a candle stuck to the brim of their cap, or to the wall. It was then hauled to the surface on wooden sledges pulled by a chain attached to a capstan, which was turned by a pony or donkey harnessed to the end of a long, wooden lever – or 'spack'. The animal would walk round and round in a circle, and an experienced animal would keep its eye open and stop, automatically, when the sledge reached the top.

The stone was collected by horse-drawn waggons (known as 'carts') which made a tremendous din as they thundered down the narrow streets of Swanage towards the seafront in a cloud of dust. Swanage builder and historian William Masters Hardy, described how the stone-carrying waggons (sometimes as many as 50 a day) created ruts in the roads, which were 'nine and ten inches deep.'

Mining a cliff-side quarry, such as Tilly Whim, was a different proposition from mining inland; for here the stone was already exposed. However, in order that it could be worked, it was necessary to create a horizontal ledge on the cliff face, from where it was possible to burrow into it, great pillars of stone being left to support the roof. Blocks of stone obtained in this way were then lowered from the ledge using a derrick (known as a 'whim' and worked by a capstan and donkey) into rowing boats or 'lighters' waiting below. Whence, it was transported around the coast to Swanage. Here, the stone was taken to the seafront and stored in the open air in repositories known as 'bankers', at each of which fifty, or so, men were employed. Their task was to cut the stone into appropriate shapes for flagstones, kerbstones, building blocks, corbels, pillars, etc.; the final smoothing and finishing – or 'dressing' – being performed using chisels and the traditional round-headed, wooden mallets. So important a commodity was stone that there was a time when the people of Swanage chose to use blocks of it to pay for their goods, rather than use the coinage of the realm.

From the 'bankers', stone was manhandled into specially constructed high-sided, horse-drawn carts designed to enter the water, and manhandled again into waiting lighters. This involved men standing chest deep in water for long periods of time, and it was not unknown, in wintertime, for a man to die of cold when performing this operation.

It is not unusual, even today, after a storm for clay pipes to be washed up on Swanage beach, and one can imagine that these might have belonged to the poor, shivering stone-loaders who were obliged to smoke to keep themselves warm. Finally, the lighters ferried the stone into deeper water, to be loaded into larger sailing ships, which conveyed it round the coast and up the River Thames to London.

In 1805, when he was seventeen years old, John Mowlem left Swanage to seek his fortune elsewhere. By 1823 he had created a firm of his own, 'John Mowlem & Company', which was principally involved in maintaining the streets of the capital. In 1843, at the age of fifty-five, Mowlem retired and returned with his wife Susannah, to Swanage.

Mowlem pressed hard for Swanage to be linked by branch line to the main railway line at Wareham, but alas, he did not live to see his dream come true. Such a link would facilitate the transportation of stone (and also clay, which Purbeck contained in abundance) from the Isle of Purbeck to other parts of the country, and in particular to the capital, where it was urgently required.

George Burt, born in 1816, was John Mowlem's nephew; his father Robert, was a Swanage stonemason, having married Laetitia, sister of Mowlem's wife, Susannah. The Burts were stone and coal merchants and they also owned a bakery. Like Mowlem, Burt had served his apprenticeship in the Swanage quarries.

Mowlem appreciated Burt's 'good business qualities, shrewdness, fine character and energy of nature.' In 1835 he invited the nineteen-year-old Burt to London to join him and his colleague Joseph Freeman (a Yorkshire stonemason) at their firm. In 1844, Mowlem took Burt and Freeman into partnership and created the firm 'Mowlem, Burt & Freeman'. Their work involved improving and widening the streets of London and latterly, the construction of buildings, including the rebuilding of London's Billingsgate Fish Market in 1874.

Mowlem's dream of creating a rail link between Swanage and Wareham was only fulfilled after his death, when it was left to Burt and others to promote the railway. This required an authorizing Act of Parliament, which was passed by royal assent on 18 July 1881. Construction of the line, single track and 10¼ miles in length by Curry & Reeves of London, commenced on 5 May 1883. The LSWR agreed to manage the line.

Corfe's Village Band, circa 1910. Photo: Jim Fooks

Logic dictated that the junction for Purbeck should be Wareham railway station. However, the ancient town was surrounded by Saxon walls, and it was important that these should not be impinged upon. It was, therefore, decided that the junction should be created at Worgret, a mile or so to the west of the town.

On 16 May 1885 the first steam train arrived at Corfe's spanking new railway station, constructed by Southampton builders Bull & Son, using local stone. In order to link the station to West Street by a roadway, it had been necessary to demolish a cottage which had housed the village's museum since 1880.

> *The directors [of the LSWR] and other friends had left Waterloo in two special carriages at 2.30 and were transferred to the new line at Wareham. A stop was made at Corfe Castle to receive the congratulations of that ancient borough and the village band joined in the welcome.*

Four days later, on Wednesday 20 May, the line opened for passenger traffic and a public holiday was declared. Each day the train made five journeys to Swanage, commencing at 7.20 a.m.[1]

Now, instead of the journey from Wareham to Swanage taking 1½ hours and costing two shillings and sixpence (2/6d), it could be achieved by train in 25 minutes, at a cost of 11 pence. Said Editha Langtree

> *I remember, as a little girl, going to Swanage by train. The seats were of wood, and no tops to the coaches, just open to the skies.*

Station Road: sheep awaiting transportation. Photo: Bob Richards

February 1920: Thames, with its cargo of clergy and laypersons, en route to Goathorn for the dedication of its new Mission Church of St Paul. Photo: David Haysom

(It was intended that the tramway which ran along Swanage's seafront from the 'bankers' to the pier head, should be linked to the new, mainline Swanage branch of the LSWR. This did not come to pass.)

On 25 June 1886, the LSWR duly purchased the Purbeck line. The coming of the railway also meant that not only stone, but also milk and livestock could be conveyed by train. Adjoining the station at Corfe was a cattle dock into which sheep, cattle, and pigs were herded, prior to being loaded onto trucks. Also, heavy horses could be transported by rail to areas of the county where they were required to carry out contract work. In the station yard water was obtained from a well, and pumped to the surface by hand pump.

Paradoxically, the arrival of the railway in Swanage in 1885, together with the increasing use of brick in building construction, coincided with the beginning of the decline of the Swanage stone industry.

Early in the twentieth century the railway began to carry holidaymakers as well as freight, and Swanage rapidly developed as a seaside resort.

On 26 February 1920 clergy, and a large number of parishioners, arrived by train at Corfe Station from Swanage. From here they were taken to Arfleet and transported in open, clay waggons to Goathorn for the opening of the newly-built St Paul's Mission Church. (Goathorn being under the jurisdiction of St Mary's church, Swanage).

In 1923, the LSWR became part of Southern Railway. With the outbreak of the Second World War in September 1939, the Purbeck railway line carried children who had been evacuated from London to Purbeck for safety reasons, to be safe from enemy bombing.

In 1944 troops were transported to Purbeck, which was a training area. The same was true in 1945, prior to the D-Day invasion of France on 6 June, when the volume of military traffic was so great that it became necessary to extend the loop of track at Corfe, in order that 'up' and 'down' trains could pass one another.

After the Second World War there was a decline in both passenger and freight transportation. With increasing prosperity, holidaymakers preferred to travel in their own motor vehicles, rather than by train. And similarly, road transport became the favoured option for freight.

The signal box at Corfe had originally been an integral part of the railway station. However, in June 1956, the porters' lobby on the 'up' platform was enlarged to become the new signal box.

In March 1963, Chairman of British Railways (which came into existence in 1948, when the railways were nationalised), Dr Richard Beeching had, for economic reasons, recommended to the government the closure of no less than one third of the country's rail network. However, the Purbeck railway initially escaped closure. At this time, steam locomotives were being replaced by diesel engines. Finally, in 1965, the haulage of freight from Corfe and Swanage ceased.

From 1969 onwards the 'through train' service from London to Corfe/ Swanage was cancelled and passengers were, henceforth, obliged to change trains at Wareham.

In early 1971 the Southern Region of British Rail (formerly British Railways) gave notice that from Monday, 3 January 1972, the passenger service between Wareham and Swanage would be withdrawn, and Corfe and Swanage Stations would be closed. In fact, the last train ran on 1 January, there being no service on the following day, which was a Sunday.

During that summer, British Rail contractors lifted the entire track between Swanage and Corfe, and beyond as far as Motala near Furzebrook. Only the line from Worgret Junction to Furzebrook was kept open by British Rail for the export of ball clay (and later of oil and gas from nearby Wytch Farm).

It was not a question of simply closing the lines and leaving the tracks in situ in case a succeeding government had a change of heart. Instead, a part of the country's infrastructure, which had been created at enormous cost in labour and money, was simply ripped up. The newly-created Swanage Railway Company would dearly liked to have purchased the 6½ miles of track, but was unable to afford it. Dorset County Council now purchased Corfe's station, and leased it to a computer technology company. In 1975 the residents of Swanage voted for the railway to be rebuilt.

In 1992, Dorset County Council granted the Swanage Railway Company a lease on the railway station and a licence to restore it. The first passenger train ran in 1979 along the few hundred yards of track from Swanage which had now been relaid. The line to Herston Halt, 1 mile distant, was opened at Easter 1984; to Harman's Cross Station, 3 miles distant, in March 1989; and to Corfe Station in August 1995.[2]

The Swanage Railway Society, the Swanage-Wareham Railway Group,

The Ship Inn – *later* The Bankes Arms – *and adjacent cottage/museum, demolished in 1883/1884 to make way for Station Road.* Photo: Bob Richards

86

and the Southern Steam Group had all played a part in the Purbeck railway restoration project, and on 26 August 2001 a commemorative plaque was unveiled on the 'up' platform at Harman's Cross Station, in honour of their pioneering achievement.

The footbridge at Corfe Station originally stood at Merton Park Station on the Wimbledon to West Croydon line. However, when this line became redundant in 1998 the bridge was donated to the Swanage Railway, and suitably adapted for re-erection at Corfe. The footbridge was formally opened by David Quarmby, Chairman of the Strategic Rail Authority, on 28 April 2007.

Ada Cooper came to live at Corfe from nearby Church Knowle in 1922, when she was ten years old. The following year the family moved into their newly-built house, Higher Gardens (subsequently known as 95 East Street). In her childhood days, she said, for those who wished to travel to Swanage, say, to the theatre, the most convenient way was by train; the return fare being 8 pence. (The return rail fare to Wareham was ninepence, and to Poole, three shillings and sixpence.) This was because the main route by road to Swanage, at that time, was via Kingston and Langton Matravers, which meant a circuitous and time-consuming journey by bus. (It was only after the Second World War that buses operated on the more direct 'Valley Road', which linked Corfe and Swanage by way of Harman's Cross.) The train also conveyed senior pupils from Corfe and Wareham to the newly-built Swanage Grammar School, which opened in 1929.

It was on 15 July 1926 that a ferry service came into operation at the entrance to Poole Harbour, linking Poole's Sandbanks peninsula with Purbeck. The ferry was steam driven and carried 15 motor cars. Prior to this, the only way of travelling to Poole and Bournemouth from Corfe was by bus or by train. However, a third alternative in the summer months was to journey to Swanage and catch a paddle steamer from the pier to Bournemouth – a voyage which took just over an hour. A favourite paddle steamer was the *Monarch*.

During the summer months trains, sometimes powered by two steam locomotives not one, brought holidaymakers to Swanage. Corfe railway station was a very busy place, said Ada

> *as all goods, cattle, and anything else which had to be moved, went by train. Staff included Mr Greenstock, the stationmaster who lived at the station house; a man in the ticket office; two or three porters; and two single men who took it in turns to man the signal box above the 'down' platform. Mr Grace (who was succeeded by Mr Honour), and Mr Simkins were the signalmen.*

Above left: *Bob Richards (late-turn signalman) and Arthur Galton (early-turn signalman), Saturday 1 January 1972, the day that the last train ran, and two days before the Corfe Castle line was officially closed.* Photo: Peter Frost

Above right: *Bob Richards, removing key token for single-line track from Corfe Castle to Worgret Junction.* Photo: Bob Richards

As it was a single-track line, it was necessary to avoid the possibility that two trains might meet head on from opposite directions. To this end, a 'single-line tablet' – or token – was kept in a machine in the signal box, and only when an engine driver was in possession of this tablet was he permitted to proceed. On receipt of the tablet from the signalman the driver placed it in a leather pouch, and the signal lever was moved by hand to show green. The train could now proceed safely.[3]

In addition to movements up and down the branch line, there was a through train to London at 9.30 a.m. each day; with last train from London arriving in Corfe at about 10 p.m.

Ada Cooper often saw flocks of sheep being driven through the village, en route by rail to sheep fairs at Dorchester or Woodbury Hill near Bere Regis. Other animals which went through the village on foot in the early morning were the elephants from a circus (on their way to a performance at Swanage). They would return in the same, quiet fashion a week later.[4]

Thirteen
MUSIC AND ENTERTAINMENT; RECREATION AND LEISURE

Editha Langtree had been fond of singing and drama since her childhood
in the 1880s and 1890s. On one occasion, she travelled to Bournemouth
to hear English contralto, Dame Clara Butt (1872-1936) sing. Music was in
the family, as she revealed in her *Memories*.[1]

> *Will Orchard came in after tea of a Sunday. Reg [her brother] took bass,
> Fred [her uncle] the cornet, and the others, second cornet and tenor. I played
> the harmonium, and it was always hymns till church time [i.e. evening service].*

It was during the First World War that Editha joined the church choir, of
which she would be a member for a period of fifty years. In her early days
with the choir there were 40, or so, members. Subsequently, and not surprisingly, numbers fell until there were only two sopranos, two altos, 'no men's
voices', and a few children. The Women's Institute also had 'a small choir of
ladies voices'.

In her *Memories*, Editha listed a succession of organists, engaged by the
choir, who sometimes travelled to Corfe from afar. Mrs A. J. White, formerly
of Kingston; Mr George from Parkstone; Mr Stickland, also from Parkstone,
who used to cycle to Corfe on Fridays for practice and on Sundays for
services; Mr Alistair Tomes from Swanage, who suffered from tuberculosis
and 'came as long as his strength allowed, dying three months later after
leaving'; Mr Arthur Phillips, 'a perfect gentleman' and highly qualified in
music, being the possessor of the degrees LRAM and ARCO.

The next organist, Mr Galpin, 'played well, but never really took a
practice. He got the choirboys 4/- a year'. However, he kept the money for
himself. He was finally 'tripped up by the rector, who discovered him in the
church drinking from a bottle of whisky'. Next came Mr Chick, who 'was as
bad as Galpin, and a stranger to the truth'.

Mr Prichard, Editha described as a 'professional' organist, but he and the
rector, the Reverend Batley, fell out 'so he gave in his notice'. Mr Leonard
from Swanage, with whom the choir performed Handel's *Messiah*, was 'a
splendid help'. The organist who stayed the longest was Mr Harold Ramsey
'who could play any instrument'.

Every summer, in the month of June, the Swanage Choral Society, under

East Street, 1920s. Photo: Bob Richards

its conductor Mr Edwin Farwell, organist of the parish church of St Mary the Virgin, Swanage from 1929 to 1940, performed an operetta, usually one by Gilbert and Sullivan. In *HMS Pinafore*, Editha took the part of 'Little Buttercup'. Not only did she sing, she also made many of the costumes for the performances. 'It was the happiest time of my life', she said.

One year, said Editha, with the participation of professional soloists, the society staged Richard Wagner's opera *Lohengrin*, music being provided by the village orchestra, again 'with a little outside assistance'. Leader of the orchestra was Miss Pauline Stock, a music teacher from Bournemouth, who travelled daily to Corfe by train. In attendance was none other than Siegfried Wagner, son of the great composer, who 'congratulated Mr Farwell on his achievements'.

> *The stage was made up of beer crates, borrowed from the Castle Inn, on which were laid planks; and a curtain was slung from wires across the front of the stage. Some wonderful lighting effects were produced, too: I remember during the performance of* The Sorcerer, *there were some marvellous whizz bangs and flashes.*

On other occasions, during the summer, the orchestra played in the open air at church fêtes: for example, at Kimmeridge and East Lulworth rectories.

During a rehearsal for Shakespeare's play *Romeo and Juliet*, in the church hall, said Editha, with Ethel Dru Drury, the doctor's wife as producer, a clothes horse was used for the balcony scene. However, it was laden with wet dishcloths which the schoolchildren had used that day for cooking. Editha took the part of Juliet and her schoolfellow Hodder, was Romeo.

As he was kneeling on the floor looking up at me, I leant over and the clothes horse fell on Hodder knocking him backwards, and his face came up through these wet cloths. Sid Paine laughed so much, the tears were rolling down his face. Mrs D [Dru Drury] tried to start and restart, but each time we got to the same place, then the laughing would start all over again and eventually the rehearsal was called off.

In her 'earliest youth', said Editha, 'The fairs and circus came, and for a few pence we could see the animals performing their tricks'. Corfe held two fairs annually (fair – a gathering of stalls and amusements for public entertainment): on 12 May and on 29 October 'in The Square, and up each Street according to the amount to be sold.' She recalled the time when a dancing bear used to visit Corfe, which 'caused great excitement'. The handler sang 'Laddie Dong, Laddie Dong, etc.', and the bear danced to it. Then came the organ grinder and his monkey, who held out his hat for pennies.

Editha described how, when Canon Eldon Surtees Bankes (rector 1854-1899, who was a direct descendant of Lady Bankes of Civil War fame) was rector, he would invite the schoolchildren to the rectory for 'a treat and tea'. The girls were instructed to curtsy to the canon and his wife Charlotte, and

The Square, William Wiseman's sweet shop and tobacconist. Photo: Bob Richards

Installation of village sign 'The Gift of Four' in 1927, by Francis Newbery.
Photo: Corfe Castle Town Trust

Relaxing on 'The Halves'. Photo: Bob Richards

the boys to salute. 'I would not curtsie', said Editha, 'in spite of the school-master's eye upon us, and I got away with it. I objected to this obeisance'.

In 1902, the villagers took part in a procession to mark the end of the South African War.

Miss Card [her headmistress] dressed me as Britannia. It was a rush to get a horse and trap, and to dress the part with a gold helmet, trident etc.

Miss Cleall, whose parents George and Mary, were proprietors of the eponymously named stores in The Square, was middle-aged when Ada first knew her. 'In her spare time she played the viola and belonged to the orchestra, often having us children in her house for practices'.

Taylor Stockley, known as 'Old Taylor', played in the village band. The bandmaster was William Wiseman, proprietor of a sweet shop and tobacconist. When Wiseman was unable to play his instrument, due to the loss of his front teeth, 'he made himself some wooden ones, which enabled him to resume playing'.

When, in 1923, Ralph Bankes of Kingston Lacy ('who owned the castle and much of the village') came of age i.e. attained the age of twenty-one years – said Ada

we were given tea and a film show, and I remember some of the children were alarmed at the sight of a railway engine coming towards them on the screen, never having seen a film before.

Dances were frequently held in the school, said Ada, and country dancing in the Methodist Hall was a popular pastime; the teacher being Miss Oates from Lytchett Matravers. There were

quite large whist drives too. The one just before Christmas was always an event, when the prizes were poultry, ham, and other seasonal items.

A fête was traditionally held in the castle grounds on Whit Monday, organized latterly by members of the church.

Nearly everyone went. There were races for the children, and various sideshows, and always, bowling for the pig.

Pageants were popular: the first that Ada could recall being in 1927, when the sign was erected in the village square. Painted by Francis Newbery, it was called 'The Gift of Four' and depicted Edward King and Martyr.

On the occasion of King George V and Queen Mary's Silver Jubilee celebrations (6-12 May 1935), said Ada, 'for the first time we heard the voice of the sovereign on the wireless, speaking to his people'. In the same way, she listened to the abdication speech of King George V's successor, his eldest son, Edward VIII, which was broadcast on the radio on 11 December 1936.

Our usual way of celebrating 'joyful royal events', said Ada, such as the coronation of King George VI and Queen Elizabeth as King and Queen of the United Kingdom on 12 May 1937,

> consisted of decorating the houses with patriotic flags and banners, and having a procession of decorated floats with individuals dressed up in fancy costumes.

Organizations such as the British Legion and the Friendly Societies (mutual associations providing sickness benefits, life assurance, and pensions) 'had decorated waggons representing various themes'. The theme of the Choral Society was the League of Nations

> in which those taking part each represented a different nation. I was a Chinese, with a long pigtail. Another time, our theme was Neptune with his attendants: mermaids, sailors, and fisherman with their nets. All the competitors met in The Square, where the costumes and floats were judged, and prizes awarded.

On that occasion, said Editha, 'I did a float and won 1st prize'.

Ada occasionally visited one of the two cinemas at Swanage. 'I remember seeing Charlie Chaplin's first talking picture' – *The Great Dictator* (1940) – she said.

The Salvation Army, a Christian evangelical organization, used to hold regular services in The Square, said Editha. But in later years it was only on Christmas Day that they came to play carols: 'lasses as well as men, and they played very well'.

Cricket matches were played at Bucknowle, and the men used to walk across to the cricket pitch via Copper Bridge. Captain of the village team was, needless to say, that man of many talents, Dr Dru Drury. Little did the cricketers of the day realize, that beneath their feet were the remains of a Roman villa, which was subsequently excavated.

Although there were occasional day trips by motor coach, 'the coach tour holiday did not start until after the [Second World] war'.[2]

Fourteen
NOTEWORTHY RESIDENTS AND VISITORS

Charlotte Augusta, Princess of Wales (1796-1817)

On 29 October 1814, an eventful visit to Corfe was made by Princess Charlotte, only child of George, Prince of Wales and Caroline of Brunswick. Here she was met by George Bankes (1788-1856), 3rd son of Henry Bankes of Kingston Hall (later Kingston Lacy) – the castle's current owner. Having arrived at the castle, her Royal Highness

had already quitted her carriage, but as he [Bankes] knew the walk through its walls was a long one, he requested permission to direct that the carriage should follow, and this being graciously acceded to, the barrier was thrown down, and the spirited horses brought the carriage safely over the bridge, and as far up the hill as the steep nature of its acclivity would permit.

There was no portion of this extensive ruin that the princess omitted to visit, so that the carriage was a welcome accommodation for her return.

Subsequently, she

sat down to partake of the humble, but ample profusion of a country inn, The Ship [which subsequently became The Bankes Arms], which still holds a well-earned pre-eminence in the borough.

No one in the royal party had evidently realized that this was the day of Corfe's annual fair.

This proved to be a new source of amusement for the princess, as from the window of the little inn, she saw the lively traffic of the gay throng, taking part herself in the festival by extensive purchases of fairings [small presents] from the little booths which stood thickly arranged between the moat of the castle and the inn.

Sadly, Princess Charlotte's life was destined to be a short one. She died in 1817 at the age of twenty-one, having given birth to a stillborn son. Three years later, her father acceded to the throne as King George IV.[1]

The Bankes Arms. Photo: Bob Richards

Thomas Hardy (1840-1928)

No account of the history of Corfe would be complete without a mention of Dorsetshire's famous poet and novelist Thomas Hardy, who mentions the village of *Corvsgate*, as he called it, several times in his writings.

In his novel *The Hand of Ethelberta* (published in 1876 in book form), the eponymous hero set off on a donkey from Swanage – *Knollsea* – for Corfe

by a path on the shore... and thence up the steep crest of land opposite... Turning to the left along the lofty ridge which ran inland, the country on each side lay beneath her like a map... Thence she ambled along through a huge cemetery of barrows containing human dust from prehistoric times.

Ethelberta now descended from the top of the ridge into the village of Corfe, and having reached the castle, she

crossed the bridge over the moat, and rode under the first archway into the outer ward [bailey]. Ascending the green incline and through another arch into the second ward, she still pressed on...

Finally, after a further climb, she found herself among 'windy corridors' and 'mildewed dungeons'.

In Hardy's novel *Desperate Remedies*, young architect Edward Springrove, tells lady's maid Cytherea Graye, that he 'passed Corvsgate Castle about an hour ago'. Finally, in his short story *Old Mrs Trundle*, the curate decides to 'make a little watercolour sketch, showing a distant view of the Corvsgate ruin two miles off...'

Francis Henry Newbery (1855-1946)

From 1885 to 1917, painter and sculptor Francis Newbery, son of a Devonshire shoemaker, was Director of the Glasgow School of Art, where his wife Jessie (née Rowat), taught embroidery and design. Prior to his retirement, he suffered a nervous breakdown. He later told Swanage photographer Helen Muspratt, 'about his heartbreak at losing so many of his talented students, cut down in the trenches' during the First World War.[2]

In 1919 the Newberys relocated to Corfe, where, for the next two years, they resided at The Greyhound Inn

Infant School, Corfe, 1920, by Francis Newbery. Photo: Corfe Castle Town Trust

Francis Newbery in front of his altarpiece, Roman Catholic church, Swanage, circa 1932. Photograph by Helen Muspratt. Photo: Jessica Sutcliffe

Jessie Newbery at Corfe in 1930. Photograph by Helen Muspratt. Photo: Jessica Sutcliffe

The Greyhound Inn (left foreground), with adjacent cottage which was subsequently incorporated into it. Photo: Bob Richards

prior to purchasing a house in East Street, to which they gave the name Newbery's, and also Well Court in West Street.

(The Greyhound was originally a seventeenth-century coaching inn called The Black Dog. At some stage, the house on its eastern side, also seventeenth-century, was incorporated into it. Its porch bears the inscription 'I. C. 1733' this being the initials of the then owner, John Cockram. In the eighteenth century, a new house was erected between it and the adjacent building – now Dragons Village Bakery.)[3]

Here in Corfe, using the former chapel/British School at Well Court as his studio, Newbery continued with his painting and sculpture: favourite subjects being the castle; a thatcher and his tools; the verger of the parish church; and rural folk, including a shepherd wearing his smock.

The Well Court studio was also used by New Zealand-born painter Frances M. Hodgkins (1869-1947), and by Scottish landscape painter, Sir David Murray (1849-1933).

Amongst Newbery's other creations were 'The Gift of Four', a depiction of King Edward, which bore the inscription

EDWARD THE MARTYR: KING OF WESSEX
TREACHEROUSLY STABBED AT THE GATE OF
CORFE CASTLE BY HIS STEPMOTHER ELFRIDA 978

This, he gifted to the village, and it hung in The Square from 1927 until 1951 when it was replaced with a new sign, painted by Robin Pearce. Newbery also sculpted a statuette of King Edward for the top of the church's east gable.

To commemorate the dead of the First World War, Newbery designed the Memorial Gateway of the old, East Street Cemetery. It bears the inscription 'Do'[r]set men don't sheame [shame] their kind' (a quotation from *In Praise of Dorset* by the Dorset dialect poet William Barnes). Today, the memorial bears plaques commemorating the dead of both the First World War, of which there were 34; and the Second World War, of which there were 20.

However, two names do not appear on the war memorial plaque. They were the sons of Henry Frank Stockley, clay miner and his wife, Mary Ann (née Taylor) of Chapel House, East Street, Corfe. Both sons were single men. George Stockley (born 1889), Driver, Hampshire Battery, Royal Field Artillery, was killed in action on 20 June 1916. His younger brother Albert William Stockley (born 1897), Private, 1st/4th Battalion, Dorsetshire Regiment, died on 1 April 1920 as a result of his wartime injuries.[5]

Kaiser Wilhelm II (1859-1941)

Editha Langtree was aged twenty-five when German Kaiser visited Corfe in the winter of 1907. The children marched to The Square and

> *I had a good view of him. He looked very stern in his grey uniform and brass helmet, and we stood by Sheasby's Tea Rooms and sang our national anthem. We were unaware of his evil designs. Probably, he had them in mind then.*

Seven years later, Britain would be at war with Germany.

The Princess of Wales (1867-1953)

The Princess (later Queen Mary) visited Corfe in October 1908. She had tea at The Bankes Arms (seventeenth century, built on the site of a sixteenth-century inn called The Ship), said Editha. 'She sat at a round table' and subsequently, 'a notch was cut where she sat'.

Edith Clarke Bowen (née Neill)

Edith, from Largs in Ayrshire, Scotland, was educated at Sherborne School for Girls. She met and married Commander John Herbert Bowen of the Royal Navy, and in the mid-1930s, they couple moved to Worth Matravers. Subsequently, they moved to Well Court in West Street, where in 1958/9 they established 'Fleursec', the first dried flower studio in the South of England. Here, dried flower arrangements were sold to members of the public, and to other outlets throughout the country. Also pottery and paintings.[4]

The Taylor family
It was late in December 1943 when William Taylor, his daughters Harriet
Elizabeth – 'Beattie' – (born 1892), and Helen Beatrice (born 1901), together
with Charles Thomas 'Charlie' Meech (born 1884), his wife's son by her first
marriage, were forced out of their home in Tyneham and came to live at
Corfe, in circumstances that will shortly be described.

Tyneham was a village with about 40 inhabitants, situated 5 miles, or so,
from Corfe and about a mile from the sea. A footpath, alongside the Gwyle
Stream (pronounced 'goyle' – meaning wooded glen with stream running
through it) led to Worbarrow Bay, home to a small community of fishermen:
all of whose surname was 'Miller', and who originated from Scotland.
Tyneham House, dating from the late sixteenth century, was the home of the
Bond family.

Tyneham's one and only road was known as 'The Street', and its line of
terraced houses was known as 'The Row'. At its north end was the medieval
church of St Mary the Virgin, and its first rector was Thomas de Kingston,
who resigned from his post on 1 February 1303.

Tyneham School was established in the year 1860 by the Reverend
Nathaniel Bond of nearby Grange. Kinsman of the Bonds of Tyneham, he
was rector of Tyneham church from 1852 to 1889.

One of the buildings in The Row was Tyneham's post office and general
stores. Here, the village's one and only telephone was installed, at the time of
the First World War. Tyneham's public telephone was not installed until 1929.

The first telegraph poles to appear in the
village, said Ada Cooper, 'were made of a
rather soft, splintery, pale, grey-green wood'.

*They were magic. You could put your
arms around them, lay your head against
them, and listen (as you thought) to the
messages singing down the lines.*

Selby the postman, came from Wareham
by bicycle each day. He was succeeded by
Postman Barlow, who began with a red
bicycle before graduating to a motorcycle and
sidecar. There were no numbers on the
houses, as the postmen knew all the residents

*Helen and Elizabeth Taylor at
Tyneham, circa 1910.*
Photo: Helen Taylor

personally.
It was in the year 1902 that the Taylor
family had moved from Tincleton near

100

Dorchester to Tyneham, where father William became woodman on the Tyneham Estate. He was subsequently appointed parish clerk and sexton by the incumbent of Tyneham House – William Henry ('W. H.') Bond.

At their appropriately named home Laundry Cottages, William's wife Emily, was laundress for both Tyneham House and the rectory. Laundry Cottages was the only dwelling in the village to have running water: other householders were obliged to use the village pump. William and Emily's sons Arthur and Bert, found employment at nearby Tyneham Farm. Their daughter Beattie, assisted her mother; whilst Helen was a mere infant.

Helen Taylor at Corfe, circa 1995.

The Meech brothers were Emily's sons by her first marriage. William Meech was appointed gamekeeper on the Tyneham Estate, and Charles ('Charlie') became 'odd man' at Tyneham House (so-called because he did odd jobs).

When Helen Taylor was a pupil at Tyneham School from 1907 to 1916, Miss Norah Woodman was head teacher. In the classroom above the fireplace hung a large portrait of the late King, Edward VII, who on his death in 1910, was succeeded by George V. Beneath it was displayed a poem, which Helen had composed herself, and written out in her best handwriting:

Lost – several golden moments
between sunrise and sunset.
No reward is offered,
as they are gone forever.

When she left school, Helen took up the position of seamstress at Tyneham House.

Meanwhile, during the First World War, Helen's brothers Arthur and Bert Taylor, lost their lives; as did their step-brother William Meech. Their mother Emily Taylor, died in 1917 at the age of fifty-two. Mr W. H. Bond died in 1935 and was succeeded by his eldest son, Ralph.

On 3 September 1939, Britain and France declared war on Germany, following that country's invasion of Poland on 1 September. Prior to this, the area around Tyneham had been fortified with barbed wire, and tank obstacles and mines placed along the beach at Worbarrow.

Suddenly, in late autumn 1943, the villagers of Tyneham and district each received a letter which would change their lives. The army required an area of land which included not only Tyneham, but also the hamlets of West Creech, Povington, Worbarrow, Baltington, North and South Egliston, and Lutton for a firing range, and proposed to take it over on 19 December. A total of about 225 villagers would be evicted from their homes including 40, or so, from Tyneham itself.

Before she and her family left, Helen Taylor, now aged forty-two, pinned a note to the door of the church

Please treat the church and houses with care. We have given up our homes where many of us lived for generations to help win the war to keep men free. We shall return one day and thank you for treating the village kindly.

And so it was that just prior to Christmas, in that particularly cold winter of 1943, the inhabitants of Tyneham and district were scattered throughout the county of Dorsetshire. Alas, they were destined never to return home: the War Department having decided that the area was to become permanently incorporated into Lulworth's 7200-acre tank and gunnery range.

The Taylors (father William, daughters Beattie and Helen, and step-son Charlie Meech) now found themselves living out the remainder of their lives at Sunnymount, East Street, Corfe. But this was not an unmixed blessing because, for the first time ever, they now had indoor sanitation and electricity.

When the author visited the Taylors at Corfe he was told, by Helen, of a conversation that she once overheard between Worbarrow fisherman Henry Miller, and Mr W. H. Bond. It concerned the smuggling that, in former times, used take place at Brandy Bay which lies at the foot of the 400-foot high Gad Cliff. Here, the beach could only be reached at low tide by a special pathway created for the purpose. It was therefore an ideal place to bring in a lugger from France, in order to land contraband kegs of brandy.

William Taylor died in 1952; Charlie Meech in 1971; Beattie Taylor in 1987; and Helen Taylor in 1999. All are buried at Tyneham.

On days when the army is not engaged in firing practice, Tyneham is open to the public. The school remains intact, as does the church; although it was declared redundant and deconsecrated. Tyneham House, however, is a ruin.[6]

Leslie Everett Baynes (1902-1989)
The son of a publisher, Baynes was born on 23 March 1902 in Barnes, West London.

At the Aircraft Manufacturing Company 'Airco', Hendon, Middlesex, whose chief aircraft designer was Geoffrey de Havilland, Baynes worked as assistant to an experimental engineer. He subsequently joined HM Army

Balloon Factory at Farnborough, Hampshire, which was subsequently renamed the 'Army Aircraft Factory', and in 1912, the 'Royal Aircraft Factory' (reflecting the change in emphasis from balloons to aircraft manufacture).

In 1924, Baynes joined Short Brothers of Rochester in Kent, where he worked on the design of aircraft, including flying boats. One of his consuming interests, however, was in the field of glider design. His 'Scud I', became the first British glider (aircraft that flies without an engine) to soar for one hour. In 1933 his 'Scud II', a 'sailplane' (glider designed for sustained flight) with test-pilot, Mungo Buxton at the controls, broke the British altitude record for gliders, when it reached a height of 8750 feet. On 8 August 1935 at Woodley Aerodrome, Reading and with test pilot Dr J. P. Dewsbery at the controls, Baynes's 'Scud III', the world's first motorized sailplane, made its maiden flight.

In 1938, Baynes designed and patented the first vertical take-off and landing (V/TOL) swivel turbine 'heliplane'. This was a fixed-wing, twin-engine aircraft, with one engine at either side. For vertical take-off, the propellers would face upwards; for forward propulsion, the propellers would face forwards.

Leslie E. Baynes at Westcott Cottage, Corfe, 1966. Photo: Nigel W. E. Baynes

During the Second World War, Baynes designed an experimental, tailless aircraft for the Ministry of Supply – the so-called 'Baynes Bat' – designed to carry lightweight tanks into battle in the North African desert. He also masterminded the conversion of US-built 'Boston' bombers into 'Havoc' night-fighter aircraft which carried the Turbinlight airborne searchlight, designed to assist in the detection of enemy aircraft in the English Channel. When the war ended, in 1945, he diversified into domestic furniture, bicycle, and even children's toy design!

In the spring of 1945, Baynes married Margaret Alice Findlay, who would bear him five children: Amanda (known as 'Jane'); Susan ('Susie'); Nigel; Elizabeth ('Lizzie'); and Henrietta ('Hetty').

On 12 February 1952, Baynes filed a patent (not only in Britain, but subsequently in the USA and Canada) for his most spectacular invention to date viz. the first Variable-Sweep Fighter Aircraft for supersonic flight. However, it was left to the USA to exploit the concept of 'swing wing', which came to fruition in December 1964 with the successful launch of the General

Dynamics F-111A – the world's first, operational, variable-geometry combat aircraft.[7]

In 1953, Baynes and his family, together with their horses and dogs, became tenants of sculptor Mary Spencer Watson, at her home Dunshay Manor, situated 2 miles south-east of Corfe. The following year he founded 'Baynes Aircraft Interiors Ltd', based at Langley in Berkshire. The company, subsequently, relocated to Hurn Airport near Bournemouth, which was within commuting distance of Dunshay.

In his latter years Baynes's capacity for invention and innovation remained undiminished. In 1963-1964 he designed and patented a new form of high-speed hydrofoil sea craft which was, in essence, a combination of hydrofoil and hydroplane.

In 1965, Baynes's wife Margot, together with the five children relocated from Dunshay to Kingston-upon-Thames in Surrey. Baynes, however, preferred to stay behind in order to keep in contact with his friends. Accordingly, he moved to Westcott, East Street, Corfe, where he lived for two years. His final years were spent in Swanage.

Leslie Baynes, inventor extraordinaire, died on 13 March 1989 at the age of eighty-six. He was buried in Godlingstone Cemetery, Swanage.[8]

Rachel Margaret Lloyd (1903-1991)

Rachel was the daughter of art patron and art historian Sir Herbert Cook, and his wife Lady Mary (née Hood). Her first husband was Sir John Mellor, Chairman of the Prudential Assurance Company Ltd., from whom she was subsequently divorced. In October 1939, Rachel married William Eric Lloyd ('Bill'), an Australian who was currently a teacher at the Old Malthouse School, Langton Matravers. With the outbreak of the Second World War he joined the commandos, and Rachel worked for the Red Cross. Bill was killed during the Allied invasion of Sicily on 14 July 1943, whilst serving as Captain in the Royal Berkshire Regiment.

In 1964, Rachel decided that she wished to be nearer her sister Vera, wife of Major Douglas 'Jack' Ryder of Rempstone Hall in Purbeck. She therefore moved to Corfe, to a house at the top of West Street near the Common, which she called Osmond's, after Osmond's Farm which stood nearby.

During her time in Corfe, Rachel, a lady of independent means, developed a passionate interest in everything Elizabethan, and the first chapter of her book *Dorset Elizabethans*, published in 1967, contains details of the local pirates and their accomplices in Corfe, who operated during those times. Said she

Piracy must certainly be accounted as one of the most important Dorset industries, having its rich men even as the wool trade had. A network of

merchants and local gentry passed the goods inland from pirate ships lying in Lulworth Creek or in Studland Bay, and these found purchasers as far away as Bristol and Salisbury.[9]

In the following year, 1968, Rachel's *Murder or Sacrifice: Saint Edward King and Martyr* was published. It contains two plays, the first, *Murder: St. Edward's Fountain*, being about the death of Edward, King and martyr. It was to be accompanied by *St Edward's Song*, and *The Anglo Saxon Dirge*, which were set to music composed by her sister Vera.

Eddie O. Holland (1913-1992)

Corfe's Model Village, built to a scale of 1/20, in which the castle appears as it was prior to the Civil War, was the brainchild of Eddie Holland.

Born in 1913 at French's Farm, Lytchett Minster, Eddie was the son of farmer Owen Holland, and his wife Mary Anne (née Gover) from Corfe. When Eddie was aged two, his father died, whereupon his mother returned to her parents' home in East Street, Corfe. In 1936 he married Edna Mary Jackman of Swanage.

In the late 1950s, Eddie became proprietor of a haberdashery shop in The Square. And he owned a newsagents, also in The Square.

In the early 1960s the couple purchased Dr Dru Drury's former house, and it was in the doctor's garden, on the site where he had once held his surgeries, that the model village was built.

Eddie Holland and his wife Edna, checking on the progress of the Model Village in 1965.
Photo Ed Paris

The designer was Eddie himself, together with S. A. Walford of Parkstone. Each individual building was hand made by builder Jack Phillips (also from Parkstone), on a wooden frame rendered with concrete. The roof tiles were made from tiny fragments of Purbeck stone. The work was carried out mainly in Jack's potting shed, and the project took two years. Opening day was 7 April 1966; admission being 'Adults 2/- Children 1/-'. [10]

From the 1940s, Eddie was a member of Corfe's Parish Council, and its chairman from 1983. He founded the village's Probus Club, and was one of the founders of the Swanage and Purbeck Club. He died in 1992.

Fifteen
CHILDHOOD MEMORIES

Editha Annie Langtree was born in West Street, Corfe on 13 December 1882. Her father was Thomas, a plumber, and her mother was Elizabeth Anne, née Smith. Editha's great-grandfather Lackford Hart, had been mayor of Corfe in 1781. Editha had four brothers and one sister, she being the fourth child.

When Editha left school in 1893 at the age of eleven, she went to live with Susan Card, mother of headmistress Elizabeth Card, a widow, aged fifty-one.[1] Susan was a seamstress and she took Editha on as an apprentice.

Susan Card died in 1900,[2] whereupon her daughter Elizabeth and Editha Langtree evidently continued to live together at the family home in East Street. This was a so-called 'charity house' which belonged to Corfe Castle Charities: an organization which had originated through the munificence of Sir Edmund Uvedale. Editha (who never married) and Miss Card would live here for the remainder of their lives. 'Some of the houses in Corfe have walls made of reed and plaster', said Editha. 'A wall in this house is like that'. Editha became an apprentice dressmaker and 'after my apprenticeship days', said she, 'I was improver at 3/6 per week'.

In 1965, Editha wrote an account of her life entitled, *Memories*. She described going down, as a child, to the 'little River Wicken' with her father. He would use his spade to dam off a section and drain away the water with a bucket. Whereupon, 'we turned over the stones and caught eels, and we oft times had a bucket full'. She also learnt to milk the cows.

> *One quiet one, named 'Spark', both Reg [her brother] and I milked. He took two teats, and I the other two. It was a competition as to who should finish first. One day, I put the bucket down and when half full, Spark lifted her foot and into the bucket it went. I tried to get her to lift her foot, and in went the other one!*

Editha and her friends used to look out for the baker who would arrive from Poole 'with a basket on each arm, covered with a green baize cloth'. This was the 'muffin man', bringing muffins and crumpets. 'Mother always bought some, to our delight'.

A favourite winter pursuit, said Editha, 'was to carry water up the lane and pour it down the cart tracks'. When it froze

> *we all ran and slid down, often ending, all of us, in a heap and enjoying the fun. I could climb trees as well as the boys*

she said proudly. Editha described being taken on Sunday School outings to Studland by horse-drawn waggons. When they came to a hill, it was necessary for the children to dismount, in order not to strain the horse. This 'meant walking halfway'.

'Boys were boys in those days', said Editha, when she had become an adult. They

> *had fun knocking doors and running away. Their trick was to tie a long piece of string on the front door bell, go to the opposite side of the road, and pull it. Then, when the door was opened and no one there, the bell was pulled again.*

Editha soon got wise to the trick. 'I cut the strings', she said, 'so did not get troubled again'.

Writing in June 1965, Editha stated that recently, some boys who were playing in the castle grounds 'rolled down a stone and it hit a lady who was picnicking, and she was taken to hospital and died.'

Ada Elsie Cooper (née Fooks) was born in 1912 and came to live at Corfe at the age of ten. Her father was Arthur Leonard Fooks, a retired Royal Naval officer, and her mother was (Ada) Mabel (née Loveless). Both were born at Church Knowle in 1883. Ada had one sibling Mabel (junior), born at Portsmouth, Hampshire in 1909.

Arthur joined the Royal Navy and became a leading shipwright in Portsmouth. In 1920 the family moved to East Street, Corfe. Arthur now took a job with Marsh the builders of Wareham, for whom he also made coffins.

Ada studied creative writing and wrote poems; for example, *A Garden I Remember*, and *The Journey*.

> *A journey to the stars; what joy*
> *Free untrammelled flight through endless skies*
> *A view of earth, as of some toy*
> *While we travel forth to win the prize.*

She also wrote several anthems, including *The Bells Ring Out* and *Hear the News*, which were set to music by the church organist, Lionel Simpson.

In 1941, Ada joined the staff of Cooper's Stores, West Street (proprietor, grocer Frank Thomas 'Tom' Cooper). She took the place of a man who had left to join the armed forces, for it was now wartime. She drove the delivery van – a ten-hundredweight Ford. Her family's motor car was a Standard Ten, purchased for £170 18s 9d. In 1942, Ada and Tom were married. The couple had no offspring. When Tom died in 1960[3] she returned to her parents' house

Editha Langtree (left) with friends.
Photo: Trish Sherwood

Ada Cooper (née Fooks) and husband
Tom Cooper. Photo: Jim Fooks

in East Street, to live with her father Arthur, who was by now a widower: his wife Ada Mabel having died in 1953. Here, Ada remained until her father died in 1967. Meanwhile, Ada's sister Mabel, had married Arthur Deacon, and when he died she returned to Corfe to live with her sister.

Ada Cooper remembered how, as children,

> *we would often play in the castle grounds. There was a little side-gate which the local residents are allowed to use, so we did not have to trouble Mr Holmes, the castle gatekeeper.*

She and her family would walk to Church Knowle to visit their relations.

> *It was sometimes quite eerie coming back in the dark, as the owls would hoot in the Rectory Wood, and we were always glad to get past. One's eyes got quite accustomed to the darkness, and if it was a clear night, the stars shone brightly, and sometimes we would see a shooting star. Footpaths were not signposted then, as they are today, so unless you had local knowledge of them, they were not apparent.*

When at home indoors, said Ada, the family played card games, such as

'Beat Jack Out Of Doors', which was a favourite; also the board games 'Halma' and 'Draughts'. 'We learned Cribbage from an early age'. Every Good Friday, for some years, she and her friend would cycle to Wytch Farm

> to gather wild daffodils from a field adjoining Poole Harbour. When we got to the farmhouse, we would knock at the door and ask permission to pick the flowers, and be asked to put a few pence in the hospital collection box, kept in the porch.

Tom Cattle was born at Norden on 24 April 1924. His parents were Benjamin (foreman at the clay works of Benjamin Fayle & Co.) and Harriet (née Stockley), both born at Corfe.

When Tom was aged five his father fell seriously ill. Having moved to Parkstone, Poole for a while, the family relocated to Corfe, to the thatched cottage in West Street where Benjamin had been born. Shortly afterwards, he died. Whereupon, Tom's widowed mother found employment with Hibbs the baker, in order to support her son and his two younger sisters, Eva and Phyllis.

At Corfe, Tom Cattle attended the infant school in East Street, before transferring to the senior Bankes Memorial School across the road, where he enjoyed football, and played for the school team. 'My childhood days were always so full of marvellous things to do', he said.

> Of course, we got up to mischief, but nothing serious, apple scrumping and things like that, but the local policeman Bill Cutter kept us under control. He seemed to be always out and about, especially in the evenings. I had to be home by 8 p.m., otherwise I was in trouble. Before the electric street lamps were put in the village, the only lighting was by oil lamps so that it was quite dark. Uncle Joe Cattle was the lamp lighter in Corfe for many years.[4]

As a boy, Tom and his friend Cecil Stockley, used to visit nearby Challow Farm, where 'what we call today free range hens' used to lay eggs everywhere 'in the hedges, and on the hill in the furze bushes'. Unbeknown to farmer Wiltshire, said Tom, we

> used to collect dozens of these eggs and would take them over the other side of the hill to a disused chalk quarry.

Here, they would cook them in a frying pan on a fire, using some fat which Cecil had brought from home.

> We would cook and eat dozens of these eggs. We were never ill, nor did we get sick of them.[5]

Challow Farm, by unknown artist. Photo: Jim Fooks

As a choir boy at St Edward's church, Tom recalled scrambling into a taxi with 'Joey' – nickname of the Reverend de Kilpeck – and half a dozen, or so, of his fellow choristers, for the journey to Glebe House rectory, 'where his butler would be waiting with a slice of cake for each one of us'.[6]

As a schoolboy, Tom worked on Saturdays and school holidays for Edward 'Ted' Moss, butcher, of West Street

cycling miles, delivering meat on that old carrier cycle with the huge fan-fronted basket on the front.

Sixteen
CORFE IN WARTIME

Editha Langtree remembered how, during the South African War (1899-1902), 'two lads from Corfe volunteered'. And when they returned home they were given a welcome and 'carried shoulder high'. Subsequently, a line of chestnut trees with alternating pink and white flowers was planted at the roadside in East Street, within the grounds of the National School, in memory of the officers of the parish who lost their lives in that conflict.

The First World War
No fewer than 34 names appear on Corfe's War Memorial, as having lost their lives in that war. Numerous others were wounded.

Thomas ('Tom') Lawrence Furmage was born at Corfe on 15 May 1886. His parents were James Furmage and his wife (Elizabeth) Ellen (née Burgess), both born at Corfe. The family lived at Scoles Dairy, attached to the seventeenth-century Scoles Manor which was situated a mile or so south of Corfe near Kingston, where James was dairyman and Tom and Harry were assistant dairymen.

In March 1912, Tom emigrated to Canada and found employment on a farm near Toronto. Here, according to the postcard (depicting the Woodbine Races, held at East Street, Toronto, which he attended) that he sent home to his parents, 'there are more people than at Brickyard [cottages at nearby Lynch], or at Scoles'.

With the outbreak of the First World War on 28 July 1914, Tom returned to the UK and joined the 2/4th Battalion, Dorsetshire Regiment as Private 201390. In December the regiment set sail from Southampton for India. After two-and-a-half years in India the regiment relocated to Egypt.

On 11 April 1918 in Palestine at the battle of Three Bushes Hill, Tom received a gunshot wound to the face and lost his right eye.

On 7 August he was transferred to the Royal Warwickshire Regiment. By now, his parents had left Scoles Dairy and returned to Corfe, to a thatched cottage in West Street.

(It is likely that, prior to the Civil War, all Corfe's buildings were thatched, but when stone became available from the ruins of the castle, it was used for roof tiles. Today, only a handful of thatched roofs remain.)

On his discharge from the army, Tom commenced work for local builder and undertaker Arthur Moss, as builder's labourer, sexton (gravedigger) and pall-bearer. And when there was a funeral his employer kindly lent him a suit.

Above: *Thomas Lawrence Furmage
(front row, left) Ahmednagar, India, 1915.*
Photo: Liz Richards

Left: *Thomas Lawrence Furmage at his
smallholding in West Street, 1925.*
Photo: Liz Richards

He also worked on his smallholding, which consisted of allotments and
several fields rented from the Bond and Bankes estates. His livestock
included two or three cows, a pig, chickens, and a mule called Jack, which
pulled the hay waggon.

On 15 December 1926, Tom, now aged forty, married Marie Jessie White
(née Gould), a widow from Kingston and the couple set up home in West
Street. They had two daughters – Pamela Irene and Norah Daphne.

On his allotment, Tom grew vegetables sufficient to last all year round.
'He also grew rows of chrysanthemums', said Norah

and an old gypsy woman would call in the autumn to buy them all. How hard Tom worked, and with only one eye. I remember him making a wooden yoke for his shoulders, from a single piece of wood, with chains to carry the buckets on either side. He also made wooden rakes with wooden teeth, ready for the haymaking. Lots of people would come and help get the hay in, and several ricks were made in the field just off West Street.

Meanwhile, Tom's younger brother Henry ('Harry') James Furmage, born at Corfe on 7 July 1889, joined the Dorsetshire Regiment. He was subsequently transferred to 100th Company, Machine Gun Corps as Gunner 14992. On 20 August 1916 at High Wood/Delville Wood, Battle of the Somme, Harry was wounded by shellfire. He died the following day and is buried at Heilly Station Cemetery, Mericourt-L'Abbe, Somme, France.

Scoles, despite its proximity to Kingston, is in the parish of Corfe, which explains why Harry's name appears on the war memorials of both villages.[1]

Henry ('Harry') James Furmage, dairyman at Scoles Farm, prior to enlisting in the army. Photo: Liz Richards

Henry ('Harry') James Furmage of the Dorsetshire Regiment. Photo: Liz Richards

The Second World War

Corfe's War Memorial contains the names of 20 men who lost their lives in that conflict. One was Francis William Yorke Batley RN, son of the rector and his wife Frances. He died on 17 September 1945, aged twenty-six: 'Killed whilst flying on active service at sea'.

In late September 1938, British Prime Minister, Neville Chamberlain, returned from Munich after a meeting with German Chancellor, Adolf Hitler. 'It became obvious that peace could not last much longer, and we began to prepare ourselves', said Ada Cooper.

Corfe's infant school having been vacated, this now became the ARP (Air Raid Precaution) organization's headquarters for the village. Ada herself attended First Aid classes, and she and some others took a second examination, which entitled them to wear a St John's Ambulance badge. An 'old ambulance' was provided which was kept in a shed below The Greyhound Inn. War was declared on 3 September 1939. In the previous week some mothers and young children – evacuees from the East End of London - had arrived in Corfe.

Editha described how, when the German bombers flew overhead and dropped their bombs, some of which fell on Kingston, Bucknowle, and Church Knowle, the villagers could hear and feel the vibrations. It was early in the war when an enemy aircraft flew over Corfe Common. Just in time, before its bomb fell, an army officer recognized it as German, 'and he helped a woman and baby to lie in the ditch, so they were saved'. Editha guessed that the enemy pilot was aiming at the railway line, but fortunately there was heavy fog that day, so he missed his target.

Orders were that at night-time, there was to be a so-called 'blackout', during which all windows were to be covered with dark curtains. The air-raid warning system was very much a 'Dad's Army' affair, said Ada. We had no siren then, so the air-raid warden, on receiving the red alert, would go round the village blowing a whistle. And when the 'all clear' came, he rang a handbell. Mercifully, said Ada, the only bombs dropped on Corfe itself, fell on West Hill and did no damage.

Editha was told by a friend of Dr Dru Drury that a German officer who had lost a leg in the fighting and was now a prisoner of war, had said to the doctor, 'as I am out of the war, do tell me where Holton Heath is'. This was a reference to the Royal Naval Cordite Factory, a top secret facility nearby. The doctor was 'cute', said Editha. He knew that if he gave away this information, the German would report it back to his homeland. So he replied nonchalantly, 'That was dismantled ages ago'. In fact, said Editha, the Germans dropped no fewer than 170 bombs in an effort to destroy Holton Heath. But they were unsuccessful, largely because decoys were lit in various

places: for example, on the heath and on Furzey Island.
Said Ada Cooper

A canteen which was run by local volunteers was established in the garage of Mortons House. A number of different regiments were stationed in the area during the war, mostly on coastal defence duties.

I particularly remember the Welsh Regiment for their fine singing at church service, Cwm Rhondda *being one of their favourite hymns. They had a sergeant with a good voice who sang* The Holy City *with great fervour.*

Another important target for the enemy was the experimental radar station at Worth Matravers. However, said Editha, many guns were brought up to protect it, and

when the Germans came in with the setting sun at Chapman's Poole, all these guns were turned on them.

From Corfe, Editha saw numerous enemy aircraft in the sky and the flashes of fire from the British guns. 'It was all over in a few minutes', she said.

On another occasion, Editha was on her way to the baker's when she 'heard an awful racket overhead'. An aircraft, flying at no more that 30 feet, was about to crash 'in a patch of mangels belonging to my brother. It exploded and caught the hedges on fire'.

On 10 October 1940, Editha was returning from Wareham when she was stopped by soldiers at the 'Halfway House' i.e. the Halfway Inn. They explained that an aircraft had crashed near to Corfe's railway viaduct. Its 'engine was buried on the north side of the river' and its wheels were 'up the castle slope', she said. This was a Hawker Hurricane, flown by Robert ('Bob') F. T. Doe of 238 Squadron, RAF Middle Wallop in Wiltshire. Whilst in combat with some Messerschmitt Bf 109 fighter aircraft over nearby Warmwell, his aircraft was shot down. However, he baled out, and parachuted down onto Brownsea Island in Poole Harbour. He was subsequently admitted to Poole Hospital with wounds to the leg and shoulder. Afterwards, he was awarded the Distinguished Flying Cross (DFC) medal and a month later, a Bar. This was to add to the Distinguished Service Order (DSO) medal which he already possessed.

William Joyce, of Irish parentage, was born in Brooklyn, New York. In 1933 he emigrated to England and fled to Germany prior to the outbreak of the Second World War, throughout which, he broadcast Nazi propaganda to Britain from Radio Hamburg. The British nicknamed him 'Lord Haw Haw'. The traitor, said Editha, even 'gave out from Germany that Corfe was bombed and the castle left in ruins'. The residents of Corfe, however, knew that it was Oliver Cromwell who had blown up the castle, in 1645!

In summer and autumn 1940, said Ada, the Battle of Britain took place, in which a major air campaign was fought over southern England.

We would see large formations of [enemy] bombers going over in daylight on their way [back] from the Midlands, and we could see the [British] fighters weaving around them. Quite a lot of planes came down in Purbeck. A Messerschmitt landed intact on West Common, near the policeman's house.

This aircraft had been taking part in an attack on the Westland Aircraft Company at Yeovil in Somersetshire. The pilot, Bernhardt Demmig, survived and was taken prisoner. The radio operator was killed. The Messerschmitt had been shot down by Squadron Leader Michael Robinson, flying a Spitfire from 601 Squadron, RAF Warmwell.[2]

The evacuation of Allied forces from the beaches of Dunkirk took place in late May/early June 1940. Invasion now seemed imminent and the Local Defence Volunteers (LDV – which later became the Home Guard) was formed. Said Ada

They dug lookout posts on the end of Challow Hill and on the side of the castle mound, so they could keep observation of the roads leading into the village.

Volunteers were called for to make camouflage nets. 'I became quite adept at using the special needle and string provided', she said.

In November/December 1940, when Southampton was being 'blitzed', 'some older children were sent here [to Corfe]'.

In the months prior to D-Day, 6 June 1944, on which day the Allied forces invaded northern France, said Ada, the large houses round about, including Bucknowle and Glebe House, were occupied by US soldiers. During Christmas of 1944, a group from the church visited them and sang carols.

It was a clear, very frosty night, and they were so grateful for our visit to them, so far from their homes. It was then I tasted Coca-Cola for the first time, when we were offered some by the men.

With the approach of D-Day, said Ada, the roads in the area were

filled with tanks and other heavy vehicles, and then they were gone, and we heard on the radio that the invasion had begun. I clearly recall that day.

There was a constant hum of [Allied] aircraft overhead; we seemed to be on the flight path as they came back to this country after the first assault.

When he left school in 1938, Tom Cattle obtained permanent employment with Ted Moss, when the latter and a colleague opened another butcher's shop in Wareham.[3] In April 1940, following his sixteenth birthday, Tom enrolled in the Corfe LDV. In April 1942, when he reached the age of eighteen, he received his call-up papers and, after training, joined the Hampshire Regiment. On 9 June 1943 he married Marjorie Gee, at Corfe's church of St Edward the Martyr.

His regiment was posted to India, where Tom was transferred to the 2nd Battalion, the Dorset Regiment. He would subsequently spend eighteen months in action against the Japanese, which he described as 'the most horrific months that I had to live through all my life'.

In Nagaland in north-east India at the Battle of Kohima (4 April to 22 June 1944), the Japanese attempted to capture the Kohima Ridge and were repulsed. '85 young men of the Dorset Regiment were left in those Naga Hills', said Tom, 'killed during one of the most horrible battles of the war'. Tom subsequently sustained a wound to the head, which required an operation and four weeks of convalescence, before he could return to active service.

Tom finally arrived home in early September 1946, almost exactly three years after leaving England. Having been reunited with his wife Marjorie, the couple now joined his mother Harriet, in the cottage at 75 East Street where she was now living. Meanwhile, from Corfe's 'Welcome Home Committee', Tom received a blue leather wallet and £5 pound note, and a card signed by Mr G. White, Chairman of the Parish Council.

By now, Ted Moss had sold his butcher's business. However, Tom obtained employment at another butcher's in Swanage. In 1948, the Cattle's first child Roger, was born. He would be followed by Stephen and Julie. Tom now joined the Dorset Constabulary as 'Police Constable 282'. He became a traffic patrol officer and retired at the age of sixty-five.[4]

Seventeen
WORKING FOLK

For forty years, Editha Langtree had a dressmaking business. She also embroidered scenes of Corfe and of flowers, which she sold to Beales department store in Bournemouth. However, when a law was introduced stating that apprentices – hers included – had to be paid, she was obliged to raise the price of her dresses, 'which upset some of the clients'. She therefore dispensed with the apprentices 'and did every stitch myself, which was more satisfactory than having to stop my work to show them how to do the job, and then having to pick out what had been done'.

Whereas there were once eight bakers in the village and the bread was delivered; now there was only one, said Editha. Furthermore, when bread deliveries ceased, 'we have to fetch what we need, which is bad for old people'.

Editha described how various premises in Corfe had changed over the years. A 'good draper's' had now become an antique shop, of which there were now five in the village.

> *What was the saddler's shop is now a drug store, and what is now about to become a cake shop was two cottages. Yet you cannot buy little useful things, except in Wareham and Swanage.*

As for the curatage, this had been turned into flats.

> *In my childhood, there lived an old scissor grinder, Joey Stanley and his wife Lovely. He was the only one to have the royal coat of arms on his machine. Joey was born in a chalk pit, and died in one. We used to get him to recite*

> *The world is round. It runs upon wheels*
> *And death is a sting that every one feels.*
> *Now if death was a thing that money could buy*
> *The rich would live and the poor die,*
> *But God in his Providence ordered it so,*
> *That the rich as well as the poor must go.*

In her youth, said Ada

> *Haymaking was totally different than today. There was more goodwill and kindness in olden days and [folk] would give a hand whenever wanted.*

Above: *Joey Stanley, scissor and knife grinder and his wife Lovely, circa 1890.*
Photo: Trish Sherwood

Right: *Sheep wash at West Mill.*
Photo: Dennis Smale

Below: *West Mill.* Photo: Bob Richards

The fields were cut with scythes and then the grass was turned and turned, before being raked into heaps, loaded into horse-drawn waggons, and delivered to the villagers' homes. First, however

a long table was laid, and all the helpers sat down to ham salad and home-brewed beer, [after which] the men would sing their favourite songs, tell jokes, and have happy times.

In West Street, said Editha, animals were brought to be slaughtered: first in an open field, and later in a shed specially erected for the purpose. The proprietor of the slaughterhouse, which she described as 'a disgrace', was Walter Moss.

Walter's son Jack, achieved notoriety when he cut the ear (which bore a tag) off a pig and stitched it on to another animal – presumably in order to claim some financial benefit. His attempt to dupe the inspector failed, and he received a one-year prison sentence.

George Welstead, an old tinsmith, used to come round with his waggon. Mother used to say, 'I've broken my cups'. 'What a good job. What should I do if people didn't smash things!' [came the reply]

Welstead also sold woollen stockings at 1 shilling per pair, said Editha. She described him as 'a very honest man', who once rose from his sickbed to pay a debt of 10 shillings which was owing.

At Boar Mill (eighteenth century, on the Byle Brook, which had replaced an earlier structure dating from the sixteenth century or before), said Ada Cooper, Charles 'Charlie' Battrick, baker and miller, baked his bread

in the old-fashioned oven, heated by faggots of wood, which were burnt to ashes and then cleaned out of the hot oven, and the loaves were inserted and left the required time to cook.

(West Mill on the Corfe River and adjacent to the castle on its west side, dated from the thirteenth century. It was demolished in 1920 and the stones used to create the gateway to East Street Cemetery, which incorporates the war memorial.)[1]

Battricks also made very good dough cakes, said Ada, but Hibbs, the bakers in The Square (proprietor Albert Hibbs), was more up-to-date, and 'in more recent years, they have started making and selling fancy cakes of all kinds'. Both bakers delivered bread to the village and to outlying parts. Matters had clearly improved in this respect, since Editha Langtree's time.

At his smithy, blacksmith William J. Mitchell, shod horses. However, 'as

Above: *Bridge Street (or lower East Street): Ralph Mitchell, blacksmiths.* Photo: Bob Richards

Below: *Purbeck Garage, East Street, proprietors Victor Ford and his sister Ivy: their brother Samuel D. Ford in doorway.* Photo: the late Samuel D. Ford

motor vehicles increased in number, and horses declined, he did repair work on cars as well'. At the garage, of which Victor ('Vic') Ford and his sister Ivy were the proprietors, the former 'had a very early charabanc [early form of omnibus with benches] in which he took people on trips around the locality'.

The licensee of The Greyhound Inn was Arthur Hobbs, a retired merchant seaman who was assisted by his wife Kathleen, and her sister.

Robert T. Chipp's tea and coffee merchant and grocery shop, subsequently became Sheasby's tea shop (now the National Trust Tea Room). This was in competition with Arthur J. Goodchild and his wife Mildred, who in summertime, 'would

Robert T. Chipp's Tea Rooms (later National Trust Tea Rooms). Photo: Bob Richards

attempt to inveigle the people visiting the castle into having tea in their tea garden'. Ernest Sheasby also had a taxi firm and a charabanc, and helped by his two sons, founded a coach company. However, he was killed by one of his own coaches which crushed him against a wall when he attempted to start the engine, forgetting that it was in gear.

Miss Emily Anne Hibbs, the draper, sold

anything in the haberdashery line, such as elastic tape, sewing cotton, stocking mending, materials, hats, and many other items.

When she retired, said Ada, Mrs Ethel Wegg, who was also proprietor of the Castle Inn, took over her shop (subsequently 'Wegg & Tuck'). In the late 1950s, its proprietor was the aforementioned Eddie O. Holland, who sold haberdashery, toys, and gifts. (This is now the National Trust shop.) Holland also owned a newspaper shop in The Square (now Dragons Village Bakery).

Many villagers had more than one 'string to their bow'. Tom Moss, brother of Arthur, did 'a bit of farming' and was landlord of The Fox Inn. The brothers also had a building business, 'which prospered for many years', and they were also undertakers. Said Ada Cooper, 'often, on a Saturday or Sunday, my father [who worked for Arthur Moss] would have to go to work to make a coffin. It seemed to us that people always died at weekends'.

John 'Jack' Hatchard and his wife Maud, ran a boot and shoe shop, and

Above: *The Square: Wegg & Tuck, milliners.*
(Now the National Trust Shop).
Left: *Sheasby's calendar.* Photo: Janice Sheasby.

also sold groceries and sweets. When Ada's family made a purchase there, amidst the 'wonderful smell of leather and dampness, joy of joys', she was given 'a handful of sweets'. At Coopers stores

> *they kept a high-class range of goods, and had some beautiful old tea canisters which were hand-painted with pictures of the flowers and berries of the coffee, tea, and rice which they held. These canisters were supported on a fixture containing a nest of little drawers holding loose pepper, cloves, and other spices, and from which a pound of pepper was always provided, even during the war when it was very scarce, for the Purbeck Marblers to take across the heath to Ower Quay, to pay their peppercorn rent for the right to take the marble there for shipment.*

John W. Woadden and his wife Edith, had 'a little grocery shop'. He was a retired butler and also verger at the church. George Day and his wife Mary Jane had a china shop. He was also an undertaker. Rosie Day lived in the Town House (1585) in The Square, beneath the Mayor's Parlour and Robing Room. Here, she sold sweets and in summer made teas for the visitors, who were served in the Robing Room itself.

(Thomas) George Savage, who had a grocer's shop in East Street, had been gassed in the First World War 'and was often very short of breath'. He supplied

> *groceries and provisions, and a few medicines – as did most grocers then – a bit of haberdashery, and outside, paraffin.*

Before electricity came to the village, 'paraffin was the main source of lighting, along with candles, and it was also used a lot in cooking'.

The Square: Day's Refreshment Rooms. Photo: Bob Richards.

Mrs Legg was licensee of The Castle Inn in East Street. Living with her was her sister and her sister's husband William R. 'Bill' Blake, a motor-engineer with a garage below Uvedale House. William Blake also ran a taxi business; repaired bicycles and tyre punctures, and 'had a charger for the accumulators which were used in the early wireless sets'. It was at The Castle Inn, said Ada, that she first heard a wireless

a crystal set with 'cats whiskers', which had to be twiddled to get the reception exactly right and cut out the static. We listened on earphones to 'Children's Hour', with Uncle Mac and Uncle David.

William Thomas had his saddler's shop in East Street, where he and Fred Pope made and repaired the harnesses used by the heavy horses which worked on the farms.

Few people rode saddle horses then, but there were a lot of light carts, used for delivery work, and this all made work for the saddlers. One could also get a leather purse or bag stitched if necessary.

The landlord (name unknown) of The Ship Inn brewed his own beer
and as there were no official opening hours, there was a lot of drinking, and he met his death falling downstairs when drunk.

(The Ship Inn dated from the mid-sixteenth century. By the turn of the nineteenth/twentieth centuries it had been renamed The Bankes Arms. In circa 1930 it was rebuilt, complete with a new frontage.)

Near to the station was the 'milk factory', where local farmers brought in their surplus milk to be pasteurized and sent off to London to be sold.

As the local farmers began to produce more milk, a lorry went round the area collecting the laden milk churns from the roadside.

George S. Cleall was one of three grocers. At his stores, the old wooden floor of which was covered in sawdust, he sold meat, groceries, and provisions.

Mortons House was built in circa 1600,[2] for Edward Daccombe (1580-1635), the latter's father William, having died in 1595. The property passed down to Edward's eldest son Robert, who settled his estates on his sister Mary, and her husband Thomas Morton of Henbury in North Dorsetshire. It later passed to John Morton, their grandson.[3]

At Mortons House, the under-gardener was Mr Moore, who was assisted by Arthur Parker – 'the boy'. Ada remembered them mowing the lawn in front of the house: Mr Moore pushing, and Arthur pulling from the front, there being no motor mowers in those days.

Said Ada, Mr Gilman and his family lived at the post office where he was postmaster and his sister Miss Gilman, the telephone operator. Otherwise, few people had telephones, apart from the doctor and certain tradesmen.

Miss Gilman appeared to be on duty at all times. One would lift the receiver and ask for the number required, and she would switch one through, but if a more distant number was wanted, she had to get the Bournemouth exchange, and ask for the number herself.

There were three postmen: John Shitler, Charlie Riddle, and Jim Goodchild.

After the second delivery of mail at midday, they were free to do their own work: Mr Goodchild in the tearooms, and Mr Riddle at his boot repairing, which he carried on in what is now the museum beneath the town hall.

In East Street, opposite Mortons House, was Robert G. 'Bobby' Moss's blacksmith's shop – now known as The Old Forge. 'I can remember seeing the heavy farm horses being shod there', said Ada.

Following the death of Miss Card in 1942, Editha took in paying guests, which she found far more remunerative than dressmaking.

Eighteen
THEN AND NOW

The population of Corfe had changed little in the past 100 years, said Editha Langtree in 1965. However, whereas in former times, households comprised large families, now many were occupied by only one person. 'I know of over 50 people living alone today', she said.

> *My parents kept cows, and fresh milk was sold at 1½s. [shillings] a pint and 2 shillings a quart. I had to help deliver the milk in cans. Woe betide me if I delivered the wrong can to the wrong house. We had to work. Not so the children today.*

For this, Editha blamed the government for not allowing children to be employed to deliver milk before 8 a.m.

> *On the whole, I think people were kinder in the old days than now. Too much money and leisure, and never satisfied. Always wanting more. As children, we were pleased with a skipping rope, a hoop, or a game of marbles. Today, it must be cycles and expensive toys, which they don't take care of. In my childhood, I had little play time. I had to look to the babies [her younger siblings], and it has not hurt me to have worked hard all my life.*

Every house kept cows, said Editha: some quite a number; also pigs and poultry, so the people did not go hungry. Householders had leases, whereby they could graze their cattle on Corfe Common. At milking time the cows were brought down through the village to sheds in the villagers' back gardens. For this reason, the cottages were build so that the front door was directly aligned with the back. In this way, the animal could be walked straight through! Nowadays, said Editha, the cows were kept on farms, and the milk was sold to the factories to be treated. 'We never get fresh milk', she said, and what people did get, did not keep.

Editha described what happened when fire broke out at Church Terrace in a house belonging to a Mr Stephen, and in the adjacent bakery. Mrs Day and her baby, who were in bed at the time, were wrapped in a sheet and lowered down into the churchyard. As for Jack Hatchard, he escaped with only his prayer book.

> *Men went up on ladders and poured buckets of water on, but that was not enough. The annoying thing was that a fire engine standing by another house did not offer to help.*

126

Corfe's first fire engine. Photo: Bob Richards

This was a reference to a fire appliance that had come from Swanage. In fact, Corfe had possessed a fire engine of its own as early as 1863.

It is interesting to note that some properties in Corfe were insured against fire, but the vast majority were not. One which was, The Greyhound Inn, displayed Sun Insurance Company's plaque on its outside wall: the Sun Fire Office having been founded in London in April 1710. However, in the late nineteenth century, new legislation such as the Local Government Act of 1894 came into effect, whereby local authorities were obliged to take responsibility for fire fighting.

The Dorset dialect was gradually dying out, said Editha, but it was still heard amongst the labouring classes, 'especially the old farm workers'.

I often wonder what my mother would say to bikinis. She would be glad to return to the grave with her modest memories.

In the days of her apprenticeship as a dressmaker, said Editha, collars were made of buckram (coarse linen, stiffened with paste), covered with satin and lace, and lined.

I had a blouse with a very small, V-neck collar and revers [turned back edges]. Oh, the horrors of my mother and aunts! Their skirts were worn long to cover the shoes. I made a skirt for a customer, 6 inches from the ground. It started the whole village talking. 'Have you seen Elsie M. in her short skirt showing her feet and legs?' Oh, horrors, the world was coming to an end!

In the church records, Editha came across the entry, 'Gave three poor men out of work 6d [pence]'. Of modern men, said she, 'they are all too well off today, and too lazy to dig their allotments'.

Also in the church records, Editha came across an entry from 1664, to say that the church bells had been rung in that year. 'How different today. We have six bells and never hear them. Only one bell on Sundays'.

Editha noted that many of the allotments had been taken over and 'developed': Halves Cottages, Higher Gardens, the Village Hall, and the railway being examples of such developments. These allotments had previously provided food for the families of the village, she said.

'It costs a lot to live these days, and a lot to die'. In respect of funerals, 'when Alf [her older brother] died, his cost was £11. Mother's was £13. Miss Card's was over £20. Fred's was £53.'

Editha stated that her mother, who had learnt dressmaking, was the first person in Corfe to buy a sewing machine.

One day, while upstairs, she heard voices and looking out, saw two women. She heard Mrs Walter Moss say, 'Let's look in drow [through] the winder [window] and see if we can see this machine that can sew with her feet!

Town criers – persons employed to make public announcements in the streets – were no longer heard in Corfe, said Editha, as there was no longer a need for them. Presumably, this was due to the advent of radio and television. She also stated that it was difficult to get a man to ring the curfew. 'It is such a pity that these old customs die out'. She described how, years ago, her eldest brother and a cousin had walked to Kimmeridge and on the return journey, become lost in the fog. However, when the curfew bell was rung at 6 a.m., 'this gave them the direction of Corfe, and they arrived [home] about 7 a.m., tired and hungry. The curfews stopped during the war, and now there isn't a man with the courage to offer to revive this old custom.'

Editha recalled the days when the floors were of stone. When they were washed, sand was sprinkled over them to keep them clean. Also, rushes were used, 'but not in my lifetime'.

Editha's first social evening took place during her apprenticeship days.

Now, today, something is on every evening. Scottish dancing, embroidery classes, pottery classes, lectures, Boy Scouts, Girl Guides, youth club, church choir practice, band practice [Sadly, Corfe's village band was dissolved in the mid-to-late 1950s], choral classes when we go to different places, joining other choirs to give a performance – so you can take your pick.

Mothers with young children wore bonnets, and when hats were worn, it was quite a sensation. People always covered their heads when entering a place of worship. That has completely died out.

Water was obtained from the village pump in The Square. It was not until just after the First World War that piped water was brought to the village.

Editha described how everything had become more expensive. The bus fare to Swanage, return, had increased from 7*d* (pence) to 3/8 (3 shillings and 8 pence).

Coal, which was 1/- (one shilling) per hundredweight (cwt) in 1914, was 2/6*d* when the war started in 1939. It was now 12/-. Electricity, which was about 16/- per quarter, was now in the region of £6. A postage stamp was now 4*d* instead of 1d. Butter used to be 1/- per pound; oranges 30 for 1/-; bread 4½*d* for a large loaf; currants and sultanas 4*d*. 'Everything was cheap. The prices are now mad'.[1]

As the older generation passes away, said Editha, 'strangers buy up the old cottages, modernize them, and let them for enormous rents – as much as 19 guineas a week.

Ada Cooper came to Corfe in 1922, at the age of ten. She described her new abode, Higher Gardens, thus.

> *In the scullery there was a copper [large copper or iron container for boiling laundry], which had to be lit with sticks every Monday to heat the water for the washing, and it was also used around Easter time to boil parsnips, which were cleared from the garden at that time to make parsnip wine.*

Eastertide was also a time for pickling eggs. They were purchased cheaply from a neighbour who kept chickens, and used for cooking during the winter months, when fresh ones were scarce and expensive. Thanks to the efforts of Ada's father Arthur in the garden, the family became virtually self-sufficient in vegetables. Furthermore, in the sheltered part of the garden he created an orchard of apple and plum trees, and 'in blossom time, the bees would hum busily on the branches'. The house was

> *modern, compared with the cottages, having a bathroom and flush toilet, but with oil lamps and a coal range for cooking and heating the water.*

However, the first winters in Corfe were so cold that

> *the water would freeze in the jugs in the bedrooms upstairs. But one summer, several years later, the slates were removed and the roof was boarded and felted, which made a great improvement.*

West Street: Farmer Reginald Stephen Langtree, bringing home the cows.
Photo: Trish Sherwood

In 1935, when electricity first came to Corfe, the event was heralded with great excitement. The company's marketing manager was sent round to each house

> *to see if we wanted electricity, and if so, to advise on what we should need in the way of light and power points. We, of course, had no idea of what we might require in the future, as apart from an electric cooker, kettle, and a little electric fire, there was little else available. Refrigerators, washing machines, toasters, mixers, and all the other gadgets of modern living were unheard of. It made a great difference to our lives when we were able to switch on the lights and acquire an electric cooker.*

Ada related how her Uncle Fred had died of tuberculosis when only a young man. It was her belief that he had contracted the disease either from animals sent to the slaughterhouse in West Street, or from drinking milk. In those days, 'there was no testing of animals, or compulsory treatment of milk [pasteurization], which was sold locally, warm from the cow'. (In the village, there were two farmers with herds of cows, Reginald Stephen Langtree and Arthur Moss.)

In The Square, on the opposite side of the church gate to the Mayor's Robing Room, was the Reading Room (which subsequently became Lloyds Bank and is now a jeweller's shop).

Here, the lads and young men went in the evenings to play cards and billiards in the upstairs room. The Reading Room was run by a committee of members, but after the 1939-45 war, the use of it gradually died, and it was closed.

The first Ada ever heard of supermarkets, she said, was near the end of the war

when a doctor friend and his wife, who had been to the USA, came and told us about these wonderful shops when you helped yourself.

In the 1930s and 1940s, the tradespersons gradually changed from horses to motor vans. And in the post-war years on the farms, horses were increasingly being replaced by tractors

old Mr Crofts of Vineyard Farm being the last man in that neighbourhood to keep one or two carthorses. Cars became more common, and people began to go out of the village to do the shopping, especially after supermarkets started, with their price cutting. Television made great strides in the late forties, and some people had a set on which to watch the coronation of Queen Elizabeth II in 1953.

Ada reflected on how life had changed in her lifetime.

First, the road, empty except for an occasional horse and cart in 1922. Today, thronged with so many cars it is a job in summer to cross to the other side. [This was on account of the influx of tourists] Shops, where you help yourself and then have to queue at the pay-out because there are never enough staff on duty; and the loss of personal service, and the lack of contact between seller and buyer.

Now that the older children go to school in Wareham, the teachers do not live in the village, so contact is lost and the school is no longer such an important part of village life as it once was. The rector has four parishes, instead of one, and although he has the help of lay assistants, things are different from the time there was a rector for each parish, and a curate or two in Corfe Castle.

Many people have retired here from town and city, and many join in village life; but there is still the feeling of 'them and us', between the old village inhabitants and the newcomers. The holiday cottage is of no help to local life, with houses standing empty during the winter months and visitors staying only one or two weeks, contributing little to the life of the village.[2]

EPILOGUE

Over the centuries, many different sounds have echoed in and around Corfe and its castle: the war cries of Viking raiders; the moans of French knights as they starved to death in the castle dungeons; the tap, tap, tap of medieval masons, as they fashioned pillars and effigies of Purbeck marble with their wooden mallets and iron chisels; cannon fire and musket fire, during the Civil War; the first steam train giving a hoot as it arrived at Corfe Station in 1885; church bells sounding the curfew; and today, the excited chattering of tourists, and the click, click, click of their cameras.

When Henry John Ralph Bankes of Kingston Lacy died in 1981, he bequeathed his house and estate, together with Corfe Castle and his 16,000-acre estate in Purbeck, to the National Trust.

Whereas, in times past Corfe reverberated to the sound of horses' hooves, today the only horses to be found in the vicinity of the village reside on the Common. Here, a friendly eye is kept upon them by the 'hayward', who is responsible for checking on the general wellbeing of the animals and also that the surrounding fences are kept in good repair.

Corfe Common: Trish Sherwood and husband Alan, 2016.

NOTES

1 The Environs of Corfe
1. Calkin, J. Bernard, *Ancient Purbeck*.
2. Lewer, David, and Dennis Smale, *Swanage Past*, pp.9-11.
3. *The Roman Villa near Corfe Castle, Dorset. Archaeological Features and Finds. A 4-year Calendar (1994-1997).*

2 Notable Events that Occurred at Corfe during the Reigns of Various Monarchs
1. Bankes, George, *The Story of Corfe Castle, and of Many Who Have Lived Here*, p.1.
2. Ibid, p.2.
3. Ibid, p.3.
4. Ibid, p.4.
5. Stevenson, Angus, and Maurice Waite, *Concise Oxford Dictionary*.
6. Bankes, George, op. cit., pp.1-4.
7. *An Inventory of Historical Monuments in the County of Dorset*, Volume Two, Part 1, p.58.
8. Ibid, p.71.
9. Bullen, Annie, *Corfe Castle*, National Trust, 2015, p.32.
10. *An Inventory of Historical Monuments in the County of Dorset*, op. cit., p.58.
11. Bullen, Annie, op. cit., p.11.
12. Ibid, p.25.
13. Shipp, W., and J. W. Hodson (editors), *The History and Antiquities of the County of Dorset*, Volume 1, p.489.
14. *An Inventory of Historical Monuments in the County of Dorset*, op. cit., p.58.
15. Shipp, W., and J. W. Hodson (editors), op. cit., p.501.
16. Bond, Thomas, *History and Description of Corfe Castle in the Isle of Purbeck, Dorset*, pp.10-11.
17. Ibid, pp.12-13.
18. Ibid, p.17.
19. Ibid, p.19.
20. Ibid, p.19.
21. Ibid, p.15.
22. Ibid, p.20
23. Shipp, W., and J. W. Hodson (editors), op. cit., p.490.
24. *An Inventory of Historical Monuments in the County of Dorset*, Volume Two, Part 1, op. cit., p.62.
25. Shipp, W., and J. W. Hodson (editors), op. cit., pp.489-90.
26. Ibid, pp.490-1.
27. *An Inventory of Historical Monuments in the County of Dorset*, Volume Two, Part 1, op. cit., p.62.
28. Bullen, Annie, op. cit., p.26.
29. *An Inventory of Historical Monuments in the County of Dorset*, Volume Two, Part 1, op. cit., p.58.
30. Bullen, Annie, op. cit., pp.32-3.
31. Bond, Thomas, *History and Description of Corfe Castle in the Isle of Purbeck*, op. cit., p.25.
32. Ibid, p.22.
33. Ibid, p.24.
34. Stevenson, Angus, and Maurice Waite, op. cit.
35. Ibid.
36. Shipp, W., and J. W. Hodson (editors), op. cit., pp.96-9.
37. *An Inventory of Historical Monuments in the County of Dorset*, Volume Two, Part 1, op. cit., p.63.
38. Shipp, W., and J. W. Hodson (editors), op. cit., p.469, note b.
39. Bond, Thomas, *History and Description of Corfe Castle in the Isle of Purbeck,* p.26.
40. Bankes, George, op. cit., p.33.
41. Shipp, W., and J. W. Hodson (editors), op. cit., p.472.
42. Ibid, p.482.

3 The Purbeck Marble Industry

1. Norris, Geoffrey, 'An Engineering Perspective on the Industrial Archaeology of the Purbeck Stone Industry'.
2. Stevenson, Angus, and Maurice Waite, *Concise Oxford Dictionary*.
3. Information kindly supplied to the author by Trelevan Haysom.
4. Information kindly supplied to the author by the late Mary Spencer Watson.
5. Short, Bernard C., *The Isle of Purbeck*, p.30.
6. Saville, R. J. (transcriber and annotator) *Ancient Order of Purbeck Marblers and Stonecutters*.
7. Weinstock, M. B., *Old Dorset*, p.160.
8. Norris, Geoffrey, op. cit.

4 Religious Worship

1. *St Edward the Martyr, Corfe Castle, The Church of, Guide and History*, William Pitfield, Dorchester.
2. Wright, C. E., *The Cultivation of Saga in Anglo-Saxon England*, p.162.
3. Ibid, p.162.
4. Ibid, pp.163-4.
5. Malmesbury, William of, *Gesta Regnum*.
6. Bond, Thomas, *History and Description of Corfe Castle in the Isle of Purbeck, Dorset*, pp.7-9.
7. Haywood, Louise, *The Town and Borough of Corfe Castle: A Walk around the Village*, p.11.
8. Shipp, W., and J. W. Hodson (editors), *The History and Antiquities of the County of Dorset*, Volume I, p.542.
9. Ibid, p.541.
10. Ibid, p.506.
11. Ibid, p.539.
12. Gough, Richard, and John Bowyer Nicholls, *The History and Antiquities of the County of Dorset*, Second Edition, Volume 1, pp.306-7.
13. Shipp, W., and J. W. Hodson (editors), op. cit., p.540.
14. Ibid, p.540.
15. *Church of St Edward, King & Martyr, Corfe Castle, Dorset: History of the Bells and Bellframe, Corfe Castle, Dorset*, Church Belfry Fund, 1995, p.15
16. Ibid, p.4.
17. Ibid, p.5.
18. Ibid, P.7.
19. Shipp, W., and J. W. Hodson (editors), op. cit., p.542.
20. *An Inventory of Historical Monuments in the County of Dorset*, Volume Two, Part 1, p.82.
21. Langtree, Editha Annie, *Memories*.
22. Cooper, Ada, *As I Remember Corfe Castle Village: 1920-1950*.
23. Cattle, Tom, *The Road from Corfe to Kohima and Beyond*.
24. Stevenson, Angus, and Maurice Waite, *Concise Oxford Dictionary*.
25. Densham, William, and Joseph Ogle, *The Story of the Congregational Churches of Dorset, from their Foundation to the Present Time*.
26. Stevenson, Angus, and Maurice Waite, *Concise Oxford Dictionary*.
27. Densham, William, and Joseph Ogle, op. cit.
28. Ibid.
29. Stevenson, Angus, and Maurice Waite, op. cit.
30. Haywood, Louise, op. cit., p.9.
31. Morgan, Kenneth O., *The Oxford Illustrated History of Britain*, p.450.
32. Densham, William, and Joseph Ogle, op. cit.
33. Haywood, Louise, op. cit., p.1.
34. Ibid, p.14.
35. Ibid, p.14.
36. Ibid, p.14.

37. Ibid, p.13.
38. Stevenson, Angus, and Maurice Waite, op. cit.
39. Haywood, Louise, op. cit., p.15.
40. Information kindly supplied by Mary Wills.

5 Corfe and the Elizabethan Pirates
1. Lloyd, Rachel, *Dorset Elizabethans*, p.31.
2. Ibid, p.20.
3. Ibid, p.33.
4. TNA HCA (High Court of Admiralty) 1/42.
5. TNA HCA 16v-8v.
6. Lloyd, Rachel, op. cit., p.45.
7. Ibid, pp.46-7.
8. Ibid, p.47.
9. Ibid, p.48.
10. Ibid, p.48.
11. Ibid, p.44.
12. Ibid, p.55.
13. HCA, 14/22.

6 Corfe Castle and the Bankes Family
1. Urban, Sylvanus, *The Gentleman's Magazine*, 1853, p.360.
2. *Mercurius Rusticus*, contemporary account of events leading up to the siege of Corfe Castle, in Hutchins, Volume I, pp.504-7.

7 The Siege
1. Shipp, W., and J. W. Hodson (editors), *The History and Antiquities of the County of Dorset*, Volume I, p.506.
2. *Mercurius Rusticus*, contemporary account of events leading up to the siege of Corfe Castle, in Hutchins, Volume I, pp.504-7.
3. Bankes, George, *The Story of Corfe Castle, and of Many Who Have Lived Here*, pp.191-2.
4. Ibid, pp.194-5
5. Ibid, p.210.
6. Ibid, p.211.
7. Ibid, p.214.
8. Ibid, p.215.
9. Sprigge, Joshua, *Anglia Rediviva*, 1674, P.III.
10. Bankes, George, op. cit., pp.214-9.
11. *An Inventory of Historical Monuments in the County of Dorset*, Volume Two, Part 1, p.19.
12. Bankes, George, op. cit., p.220.
13. Ibid, Bankes, pp.223-4.
14. Gardiner, Samuel Rawson, *The Constitutional Documents of the Puritan Revolution*, Clarendon Press, Oxford, 1889. pp.282-3.
15. Bankes, George, op. cit., p.244.
16. Ibid, p.246.
17. Ibid, p.245.
18. Ibid, p.247.
19. Ibid, p.249.
20. Ibid, p.251.

8 The Clay Industry
1. William Morton Pitt, survey, 1790.
2. The lease was renewed in October 1832, this time from Robert Davy of Ringwood, Gentleman. Dorset History Centre, D/SEN/15/1/8,10.
3. Legg, Chris, *Fayle's Tramways: Clay Mining in Purbeck*, p.15.
4. Information kindly provided by the Purbeck Mineral and Mining Museum, Norden.
5. Kidner, R. W., *The Railways of Purbeck*, p.41.
6. Church Knowle: parish registers, census records, and monumental inscriptions, church of St Peter.
7. Approximate date.
8. Meates, Joyce, *Goathorn, Studland, Dorset: A Forgotten Clayworking Community*, p.10.
9. *Blue Pool, The*, p.11.
10. Ibid, p.12.
11. Legg, Chris, op. cit., p.57.
12. 1901 Census, Corfe Castle.
13. Davies, W. J. K., *Pike Bros., Fayle & Co., Ltd.*, pp.2-3.
14. Hyland, Paul, *Purbeck: The Ingrained Island*, p.55.
15. Meates, Joyce, op. cit., p.92.
16. Leonard Gaskell Pike died in 1939.
17. Hyland, Paul, op. cit., p.55.

9 The Influence of William Morton Pitt
1. Gough, Richard, and John Bowyer Nicholls, *The History and Antiquities of the County of Dorset*, Second Edition, Volume 1, p.613.
2. Ibid, pp.306-11.
3. Stevenson, Angus, and Maurice Waite, *Concise Oxford Dictionary*.
4. Haywood, Louise, *The Town and Borough of Corfe Castle: A Walk around the Village*, p.8.
5. Shipp, W., and J. W. Hodson (editors), *The History and Antiquities of the County of Dorset*, Volume I, Hutchins, p.543.
6. The Administrators of Medical Relief to the Poor under the Poor Law Amendment Act (1834), Sherwood, Gilbert, and Piper, London, 1842, p.134.
7. Corfe Castle, Tithe Map, 1844.
8. Corfe Castle, Tithe Map, key, 1844.

10 Education
1. *A Digest of Parochial Returns*, Volume I, House of Commons, 1 April 1819.
2. Cooper, Ada, *As I Remember Corfe Castle Village: 1920-1950*.
3. The Reverend Yorke Batley died on 3 April 1960.
4. *The Railway Magazine*, 3 May, 1934.
5. Hyland, Paul, *Purbeck: The Ingrained Island*, p.55.
6. Meates, Joyce, *Goathorn, Studland, Dorset: A Forgotten Clayworking Community*, p.186.
7. Ibid, pp.210-2.
8. Densham, William, and Joseph Ogle, *The Story of the Congregational Churches of Dorset, from their Foundation to the Present Time*.
9. Ibid.
10. Ladle, Lilian, and Keith Jarvis, *Explore Corfe Village*, p.22.

11 Health Provision
1. 1911 Census, Corfe Castle.
2. Information kindly supplied by Stephen Dr Drury.
3. Langtree, Editha Annie, *Memories*.

12 The Railway
1. Lewer, David, and Dennis Smale, *Swanage Past*, pp. 133-135.
2. Green, David, (editor), *Swanage Railway: A Pictorial Guide*, Swanage Railway Company Ltd, Swanage, Dorset, 1997.
3. Information kindly supplied by Bob Richards.
4. Cooper, Ada, *As I Remember Corfe Castle Village: 1920-1950*.

13 Music and Entertainment: Recreation and Leisure
1. Langtree, Editha Annie, *Memories*.
2. Cooper, Ada, *As I Remember Corfe Castle Village: 1920-1950*.

14 Noteworthy Residents and Visitors
1. Bankes, George, *The Story of Corfe Castle, and of Many Who Have Lived Here*, pp.264-5.
2. Sutcliffe, Jessica, *Face: Shape and Angle*, p.40.
3. Haywood, Louise, *The Town and Borough of Corfe Castle: A Walk around the Village*, p.3.
4. Information kindly supplied by Liz and Bob Richards.
5. Corfe Castle, Roll of Honour, compiled by Martin Edwards, and 2003 and 1911 Censuses, Corfe Castle.
6. Norman, Andrew, *Tyneham: A Tribute*.
7. The General Dynamics F-111A made its debut flight from Fort Worth, Texas on 21 December 1964 with its wings fixed at a sweepback angle of 26 degrees. The following month it made its first flight with the wings at varying angles of sweepback, ranging from 16 to 72.5 degrees. The aircraft went into service with the U.S. Air Force and saw service in the Vietnam
8. Information kindly supplied by Leslie Everett Baynes and Nigel W. E. Baynes
9. Lloyd, Rachel, *Murder or Sacrifice: Saint Edward King and Martyr*, p.4.
10. Information kindly supplied by Ed Paris.

15 Childhood Memories
1. Edward Card died in 1863, aged 26.
2. Susan Ann Card died on 16 May 1900.
3. Frank Thomas Cooper died on 30 November 1960.
4. Cattle, Tom, *The Road from Corfe to Kohima and Beyond*.
5. Ibid.
6. Ibid.

16 Corfe in Wartime
1. Information kindly supplied by Liz and Bob Richards.
2. Legg, Rodney, *Dorset's War Diary*, p.97.
3. Cattle, Tom, *The Road from Corfe to Kohima and Beyond*.
4. Ibid.

17 Working Folk
1. Haywood, Louise, *The Town and Borough of Corfe Castle: A Walk around the Village*, p.5.
2. *An Inventory of Historical Monuments in the County of Dorset*, Volume Two, Part 1, p.
3. Shipp, W., and J. W. Hodson (editors), *The History and Antiquities of the County of Dorset*, Volume I, p.510.

18 Then and Now
1. Langtree, Editha Annie, *Memories*.
2. Cooper, Ada, *As I Remember Corfe Castle Village: 1920-1950*.

BIBLIOGRAPHY

An Inventory of Historical Monuments in the County of Dorset, Volume Two, Part 1, Royal Commission on Historical Monuments (RCHM), Her Majesty's Stationary Office, 1970.

Bankes, George, *The Story of Corfe Castle, and of Many Who Have Lived Here*, John Murray, London, 1853.

Bond, Thomas, *History and Description of Corfe Castle in the Isle of Purbeck, Dorset*, Edward Stanford, London, 1883.

Bullen, Annie, *Corfe Castle*, National Trust, 2015

Calkin, J. Bernard, *Ancient Purbeck*, Friary Press, Dorchester, 1968.

Cattle, Tom, *The Road from Corfe to Kohima and Beyond.* (Privately published).

Church of St Edward, King & Martyr, Corfe Castle, Dorset: History of the Bells and Bellframe, Corfe Castle, Dorset, Church Belfry Fund, 1995.

Cooper, Ada, *As I Remember Corfe Castle Village: 1920-1950*, Ada Cooper, 1995.

Davies, W. J. K., *Pike Bros., Fayle & Co., Ltd.*, Furzebrook (Narrow-Gauge Railway Society Handbook No. 1), 1961.

Densham, William, and Joseph Ogle, *The Story of the Congregational Churches of Dorset, from their Foundation to the Present Time*, W. Mate and Sons, Bournemouth, 1899.

Faulkner, Kenneth, *Mary Burt went for a Walk: the Story of Purbeck Methodism.*

Gough, Richard, and John Bowyer Nicholls, *The History and Antiquities of the County of Dorset*, Second Edition, John Nichols, London 1796.

Green, David, (editor), *Swanage Railway: A Pictorial Guide*, Swanage Railway Company Ltd, Swanage, Dorset, 1997.

Hawtrey, Florence M., *The History of the Hawtrey Family*, George Allen, London, 1903.

Haywood, Louise, *The Town and Borough of Corfe Castle: A Walk around the Village*, Corfe Castle Town Trust, 2015.

Hyland, Paul, *Purbeck: The Ingrained Island*, Dovecote Press, Stanbridge, 1989.

Kidner, R. W., *The Railways of Purbeck*, The Oakwood Press, Usk, Monmouthshire, 2000.

Ladle, Lilian, and Keith Jarvis, *Explore Corfe Village*, Lilian Ladle and Keith Jarvis, 1988.

Langtree, Editha Annie, *Memories*, June 1965, kindly supplied by Trish Sherwood.

Legg, Chris, *Fayle's Tramways: Clay Mining in Purbeck*, Twelveheads Press, Truro, 2014.

Legg, Rodney, *Dorset's War Diary*, Dorset Publishing Company, Wincanton, Somerset, 2004.

Lewer, David, and Dennis Smale, *Swanage Past*, Phillimore, Chichester, West Sussex, 1994.

Lloyd, Rachel, *Dorset Elizabethans*, John Murray, London, 1967.

Lloyd, Rachel, *Murder or Sacrifice: Saint Edward King and Martyr*, Rachel Lloyd, 1968.

Malmesbury, William of, *Gesta Regnum.*

Meates, Joyce, *Goathorn, Studland, Dorset: A Forgotten Clayworking Community.* Purbeck View Publishing, Worth Matravers, 2014.

Morgan, Kenneth O., *The Oxford Illustrated History of Britain*, Guild Publishing, London, 1986.

Norman, Andrew, *Tyneham: A Tribute*, Halsgrove, Wellington, Somerset, 2007.

Wilcox, W. A. (editor), *The Railway Magazine*, The Railway Publishing Company, London, 1934.

Roman Villa near Corfe Castle, Dorset, The: Archaeological Features and Finds: A 4-year Calendar (1994-1997).

Shipp, W., and J. W. Hodson (editors), *The History and Antiquities of the County of Dorset*, E. P. Publishing Ltd in collaboration with Dorset County Library, 1973.

Short, Bernard C., *The Isle of Purbeck*, J. Looker, Poole, 1967.

St Edward the Martyr, Corfe Castle, The Church of, Guide and History, William Pitfield, Dorchester.

Stevenson, Angus, and Maurice Waite, *Concise Oxford Dictionary*, Oxford University Press, New York.

Sutcliffe, Jessica, *Face: Shape and Angle*, Manchester University Press, 2016.

Shipp, W., and J. W. Hodson (editors), *The History and Antiquities of the County of Dorset* by John Hutchins, E. P. Publishing Ltd in collaboration with Dorset County Library, 1973.

Urban, Sylvanus, *The Gentleman's Magazine*, John Bowyer Nicholas, London, 1853, p.360.

Weinstock, M. B., *Old Dorset*, David & Charles, Newton Abbot, 1967.

Wright, C. E., *The Cultivation of Saga in Anglo-Saxon England*, Oliver and Boyd, Edinburgh, 1939.

INDEX